Victorious

Also by Cathy McIntosh

Finding Joy in the Journey: Savoring the Fruit of the Spirit

Victorious

Finding Triumph

When Hope Seems Lost

By Cathy McIntosh

Publishing
SW

Victorious

Finding Triumph When Hope Seems Lost

© 2016 Cathy McIntosh

SW Publishing is an imprint of Strengthened by the Word Ministries in Brighton, Colorado.

Cover image by Colourbox.

ISBN: 978-0692770047

For my friend, Sandi.
Our greatest victories are in Christ.
Trust him. He adores you.

Table of Contents

Acknowledgments

"Praise the God and Father of our Lord Jesus Christ, who has blessed us in Christ with every spiritual blessing in the heavens" (Eph. 1:3).

The Lord's specific call to the book of Esther came with profound hunger and thirst for applicable truth that he filled to overflowing. My time in study was a gift that involved sitting at the Lord's feet, enjoying his presence, and reveling at the mastery and wholeness of the Scriptures. His Word has performed a marvelous work in me and *Victorious* is a conveyance of that work. I pray it goes forth with the power of the Holy Spirit and becomes an instrument of life-changing blessing to all who read it.

Many friends played active roles in this project:

Deborah Flanagan is a powerful, steadfast intercessor and encourager. The fingerprints of her unceasing prayer covering are all over this work. I am eternally thankful for our divinely appointed friendship.

I wish to express great appreciation to those in the women's life group of Prairie Community Church, along with Jessica Dodero, Nolie Espinoza, Rochelle Hill, and Deborah Flanagan. These women read and studied *Victorious* in its infancy. I subjected them to underdeveloped thoughts, embarrassing typos, mixed metaphors, and atrocious grammar. Their comments and feedback enhanced the finished product.

Deb Hall at The Write Insight provided incredible attention to detail and grace-filled editing. Her involvement helped polish *Victorious* to a joyful shine. I'm thankful for her oversight and hope for many years of serving the Lord together.

To my family:

Michael, your unwavering support and belief in what the Lord can do through this mess of a servant help move my craziest dreams to a point of reality. Thank you for sharing every part of life with me. I love you with all I am.

Taylor, your energy and passion can spur anyone into action. I'll never forget the day I felt particularly overwhelmed with the work ahead of me and you said, "Well, just knock it out!" And so I did. Thank you for never letting me give up.

Dean, you complete my precious daughter. Thank you for loving her so fully and generously sharing her with me.

Christopher, please know that you inspire me every single day. Thanks for answering random questions by text message and for your willingness to read and comment on pages of material on the spot. You have wisdom beyond your years.

Nikki, you are my daughter in heart and I love the joy you create in my beloved son. Thank you for joining our imperfect but filled-to-the-brim-with-love family. I can't wait for the "big day"!

Finding Triumph

It's not often that we think of "finding" triumph as this book's subtitle suggests. We might believe we achieve or earn triumph, but we rarely consider discovering it. The truth is, there are times when a victory isn't obvious and we must seek it to find it.

Throughout the book of Esther, there are plot twists and turns and unexpected outcomes. And so it is with life. When situations occur, we try to anticipate the outcome by envisioning possible scenarios. We imagine what victory will look like. But when our own plot twists bring conclusions we didn't expect, we may not consider victory at all. We might even believe we've failed.

Over nearly two decades of mentoring, teaching, coaching, and ministering to women, I've met some who couldn't see their triumph because they felt trapped by disappointments and held captive by past heartache. One woman once told me that she could never share her story with others because there was no good in it. But there's good in every story. And we don't have to allow our past to keep us from finding that good.

By learning to take negative thoughts captive, practice gratitude, and embrace God's victory, we can all learn to recognize that through and even *because* of our trials, we find triumph. Our rearview mirrors show us how our trials brought such blessings as a life with Christ, delightful children, deep friendships, restored mental and physical health, freedom from addictions, husbands devoted to the Lord, supportive church families, miraculous provision of every material need, and many, many more.

In order to embrace victory, we must cling tight to the truths of Scripture and let the Word of God fill our hearts and minds. When we do, we can begin to see ourselves as God's beloved children.

Since triumph frequently looks different from long-held hopes and dreams, it's not always easy to recognize. However, when disciplines develop, when we regularly study the Bible and begin to delight ourselves in the Lord, he molds our desires and reshapes our longings, fashioning them to match his will for us. Life transformation through Scripture is a gentle and unhurried process. As I walk alongside others, it's a joy to see faith that gradually strengthens. It's deeply satisfying when God brings freedom from the bondage of past shame, regret, and deep pain.

When we earnestly seek triumph and when God opens our eyes to see it, we can embrace it with vivacity. We can see ourselves as victorious.

Personal transformation through Scripture is a continuous process. As I studied and wrote *Victorious*, my journey into God's Word was profound, to say the least. This particular dive into the Bible brought new life transformation. Over many months, God elected to use Queen Esther's history to capture my heart and mind. In the future, I trust he'll use other aspects of his Word to continue his work in me.

In my first book, *Finding Joy in the Journey: Savoring the Fruit of the Spirit*, I believe the Lord was preparing the soil, so to speak, making me ready to move deeper into the role of Bible teacher. He was teaching the teacher, which I pray and trust he will never stop doing.

Now, with *Victorious*, he has given me an entirely new experience of freedom, courage, and yes, victory. I felt the presence of the Holy Spirit join me through every step of research, discovery, observation, interpretation, application, and conveyance. I literally wept at the conclusion of this work, knowing that a deeply fulfilling spiritual season had come to an end. Discovering God through Esther brought indescribable, thrilling joy.

This is the level of joy that I desire for you: that which comes through the discovery of God through his Word. There's nothing as soul-satisfying as learning to know the Lord. I pray with fervency that you'll experience it more fully than ever before.

I pray that this study will spur a hunger to dig deep into God's Word and set aside any prior willingness to receive Bible knowledge secondhand. I hope that you'll experience exhilaration when a lightbulb of understanding shines because of careful study. After all, the Bible is God's Word written to each of us. The level of peace and satisfaction that comes through its reading will manifest in bountiful blessings when we've savored it for ourselves and put it into real-life application.

Please indulge me while I share one of the many wonderful hidden treasures I discovered through study:

Queen Esther's Hebrew name was Hadassah, which means myrtle.[1] The name Esther has a root definition that means hidden or concealed. The name Esther is also said to mean star.[2] Now, notice the crepe myrtle flowers on the book cover. There is a hidden star in the center of the bloom. I find myself giddy over such details and hope you find enjoyment in them too.

God provides his Word as a gift to his children. Through it, he offers commands and precepts that are meant for use in our daily lives. Yes, we can choose to ignore what the Word teaches, but in so doing, we rob ourselves of blessings that the Lord intends for us. God applies his Word and so must we. When we actively cooperate with him, we experience great victory, find soul-satisfying joy, and learn to recognize and embrace God's best.

If you desire to grow in your spiritual life, receive guidance and wisdom for life's joys and sorrows, strengthen your faith, increase your ability to fight temptation, find peace and comfort and a wealth of other such gifts from the Lord, including victory, then feast on the Word of God. Don't study for knowledge alone, but let it penetrate your heart. Author Robert McGee says, "As Christians, our fulfillment in this life depends not on our skills to avoid life's problems but on our ability to apply God's specific solutions to those problems. An accurate understanding of God's truth is the first step. . . ."[3]

Understanding God's Word is the first step but not our final destination. So let's also apply the Word to our lives and live it out. Our application of God's wisdom and direction to our lives brings about our ability to find triumph.

Today is a great day to start, so let's begin.

CHAPTER 1

The Powerful Hand of an Unseen God

Welcome! I'm so excited to begin this journey with you I could jump out of my socks! There is significance in that, for as I write, my hometown is under a winter weather advisory with a snow day predicted for tomorrow. I imagine you, precious reader, enjoying this book on a warm beach somewhere or surrounded by friends discussing biblical history over hot tea with your study group. From time to time, you think of me watching snowflakes descend onto mounding piles and drifts that swallow our streets and sidewalks yet willing to jump out of my cozy socks with excitement because I imagine you "here" with me.

It's a tremendous joy to study the Word of God. To partner with others in the process is a great blessing through the discussion, encouragement, and practical questions that arise. As I write, I contemplate your stories, your life situations, and ponder how the teachings will touch your faith and encourage you in hope. My aim is to lead you to examine the Scriptures for yourself, seek the Holy Spirit and his guidance, and draw out applications to use in the day-to-day—right where you are.

Please know I've prayed for you and continue to consider your precious lives as I write. I know you have faced (and may be currently facing) hard times. I have too. And so did Queen Esther. What I want you to remember and keep foremost in your minds is this: God is with you.

God is with you.

Perhaps in your current trial, you can't see evidence of his presence or discern his involvement in your life. Maybe you pray but feel like you rarely see results. Some of you walk in the bondage of addiction without receiving the deliverance you have seen others experience. Some of you face overwhelming family matters that will be decided in a courtroom, all the while wondering why God has not intervened as you've hoped. This may make you question the presence and activity of God in your life.

I encourage you to trust. And when you struggle to trust, decide to do so anyway. He cares and he's about to prove it. God is with you and I'll say again: he cares. You are his beloved child and he never takes his eye off you for an instant. He loves you more than you can imagine. He is a God who sees every smile, tear, and heartache.

Press on, sweet one, and know that the Lord holds you in the palm of his hand. Everything that the Enemy of your soul desires to heap upon you is filtered through the Lord's loving fingers. He will only allow into your life that which will strengthen your faith and mold you into his likeness.

You will get through this season, I promise. And when you trust in God, you'll get through it victoriously, whether on this side of heaven or the next. Victory is coming. As children of God, we will all be victorious.

Examining the Book of Esther

We're about to open the book of Esther and read the account of a young Jewish orphan who became Queen of Persia. Through alarming plot twists and turns, Queen Esther courageously protected her Jewish kindred from certain annihilation. She found victory and a way to triumph when everything around her seemed hopeless. If she can do it, we can too, because we serve the very same God.

Together we'll investigate characters we have never met (some we may have never heard of) and a culture we don't understand. The book may have the feel of a mysterious adventure novel, so take care to read with reverence, remembering the book of Esther is part of God's Word. Through every moment of excitement, we'll see the Lord gradually unveil his eternal power and providence. He'll prove himself mighty and afford an unlikely queen a level of victory she never dreamed possible. He'll accomplish all of this not with blatant miracles or supernatural displays but by working through ordinary people like you and me.

> *He'll accomplish all of this not with blatant miracles or supernatural displays but by working through ordinary people like you and me.*

I pray with expectation that the book of Esther will move each of us toward deeper faith, courage, and trust—even in the midst of our own challenges and adversities. I believe our journey together will inspire us to keep our eyes on what is unseen, watching for God's hand and involvement in our own lives even when he may appear absent. It is my hope that we'll learn to expect victory in our current trial and find a way to triumph when circumstances seem not entirely awesome. We'll learn to seek God's subtle fingerprints as readily as his indisputable miracles. By God's grace, we'll begin to walk in the truth that he is always at work for our ultimate good and his glory. Yes, always.

Not the Children's Version

If you grew up attending church with your family, you likely heard the story of Queen Esther in children's church. If you began, like I did, following Christ at an older age, this may provide your first glimpse into the historical account of four main characters: the orphan Hadassah (that is Esther); her cousin, Mordecai; the self-absorbed ruler of Persia, Ahasuerus; and his trusted adviser, Haman, who served with evil intent. Whether or not you're familiar with the remarkable events of Esther's life, we will not be studying the children's version. Hold on to your hats because we are about to witness an ugly and distasteful side of human nature.

Some consider Esther one of the most controversial books in the Bible. Why?

- Because God is not mentioned by name. There are only two biblical books that exclude the name of God: Esther and Song of Songs.

- There is no specific mention of God's work, nor any credit given to God for what transpires.

- There is no specific mention of prayer, the law, or the temple.

- The absence of morality and the presence of perversion are prominent components of the Persian culture.

- The New Testament neither quotes nor references this book.

- It's absent from the Dead Sea Scrolls.

- Martin Luther expressed contempt for the book of Esther, claiming that it is spoiled by too much "pagan impropriety."[1] Other scholars seem to have a reluctance to analyze it as well.

- It's interesting that Queen Esther didn't make John MacArthur's list in his book *Twelve Extraordinary Women*.[2] (I would certainly label her extraordinary).

Why Study Esther?

Yes, there are many objections to giving serious consideration to the historical account of Esther as recorded in Scripture. Even more compelling, however, are the gripping reasons to dig in and study the book for all it's worth!

- Events under Queen Esther's reign initiated the feast of Purim, which is celebrated as Jewish custom to this day. As part of the Jewish canon, the book of Esther is read annually at the feast of Purim.

- Romans 15:4 teaches, "For whatever was written in the past was written for our instruction, so that we may have hope through endurance and through the encouragement from the Scriptures."

- According to 2 Timothy 3:16–17, "All Scripture is inspired by God and profitable for teaching, for reproof, for correction, for training in righteousness; so that the man of God may be adequate, equipped for every good work" (NASB).

- There are uncanny similarities between Persia in 483 BC and present-day United States. We have much to learn from the past that can impact our present and future for God's glory.

- While God is not specifically mentioned, his fingerprints are all over the lives of Esther and the Jews. Although he seems invisible, his providence becomes obvious to those with eyes to see.

- God's sovereignty is evident, even in the midst of the ugliness of sin and immorality.

- By closing our eyes to that of which we disapprove, we miss the glory that God displays through all things as he reveals his splendor. So let's dig in and study, shall we?

We can all use a dose of hope in our morally declining world.

All of these are inspiring reasons to study this historical book. I don't care to miss a single clue hidden in the events of Esther about who God is, how he chooses to reveal himself, or the way he works through people, through circumstances, and through his Word.

We can all use a dose of hope in our morally declining world. And I've always liked a good detective novel. Let's investigate together and discover the powerful hand of an unseen God.

Where in the World is the Persian Empire?

I'm not much of a geography person, so it helps to gain a little perspective of the world of King Ahasuerus's time and compare it to the countries we're familiar with today. The king ruled 127 provinces of Persia, which is what we now know as the Middle Eastern region of the world along with parts of Africa.

If you can, pull up a world map on your cell phone, computer, or tablet. King Ahasuerus reigned over the countries we know as Libya and Egypt, the countries that surrounded the eastern side of the Mediterranean Sea, extending north to include Turkey and Bulgaria, and as far west as Pakistan. In other words, much of the Middle East as we currently know it was under the rule of the Persian king. It was a vast and mighty empire.

Where Are We on the Kingdom Calendar?

Esther begins in 483 BC, after the life of Daniel, after the Jewish exile from Judah to Babylon. Scholars place the events of Esther between chapters 6 and 7 of Ezra.

History teaches that the Jews were captured by and exiled to Babylon somewhere around 585 BC. After the reign of King Nebuchadnezzar who is prominent in the life of Daniel, Cyrus the Great (King Cyrus II) conquered Babylon in about 539 BC and issued a decree that allowed the Jews to return to Jerusalem (Ezra 1:1–4). The return to Jerusalem was gradual and many Jews remained in Persia, including Mordecai who was raising his orphaned cousin, Hadassah, who is also known as Esther.

Although many Jews were returning to Jerusalem, the time period of Esther is still considered to be within the Diaspora, which is a time when the Jews were living outside of their homeland. The time period was close to the end of the Old Testament when open miracles and prophecies were no longer common.

As we read and study, we'll discover the primary message of Esther: "God is here, even when He doesn't seem to be. God's presence in history is felt not just when the sea splits or when divine fire descends upon a mountain in full view of the entire nation. God is present in the everyday workings of life and history as well."[3] As God's children, we can trust that victory is coming whether or not we can see it on our horizon.

Through learning to recognize God's presence and sovereignty, even when he appears to be absent or hidden, we'll experience power and victory that only the King of the universe can provide. I pray this revelation will encourage us in each trial and circumstance we face as well as remind us of the greatness and faithfulness of the God we serve.

What to Expect

As we turn our attention to Persia to walk alongside Esther through her journey from orphan-child to queen of the most powerful empire of her day, we will need to keep our current timeline within focus. It's imperative that we study and read God's Word to gain not just knowledge but also a passionate drive to enrich our lives by its truth. If you complete all of the suggested reading (and I pray you do), you'll read the entire of book of Esther at least twice. Embrace the redundancy and allow yourself to steep in the Word like a tea bag in hot water.

Our goal, always, is to walk in a manner worthy of the Lord (see Col. 1:9–12) and live in ways that are honoring to him. There's no way to accomplish that without soaking in God's Word. The more we read and re-read, the more we soak.

Beginning in Chapter 2, the "From Persia to Present Day" sections will take timeless truths of the Bible and provide encouragement to live them out today. The "Digging Deeper" sections will help you glean wisdom and discernment from the Bible to bring understanding and transformation. I encourage you to devour these sections and allow the Word of God to renew your mind (see Rom. 12:2). The "Points to Ponder" sections will help you meditate on the Word and consider it through the lens of your personal experiences. These points are great for group discussions or quiet contemplations.

I'm eager to begin, aren't you? Let's dig in!

Digging Deeper

1. Read all ten chapters of Esther. Don't take time now to study it; just read it as if you're reading a novel. Get a feel for the events, the timeline, the customs, and the characters. We'll dig deeper as we progress through our time together. This reading will provide a start-to-finish overview of the book, which will prove important as we study. For now, enjoy the

irony, suspense, and subtle humor. Allow yourself to engage in the drama as it unfolds.

Some have asked about watching a movie about Esther. Feel free to do so—but only after you've read the text for yourself. Hollywood tends to take creative license, and we want to be grounded in truth. If I'm honest, my favorite movie version so far (I haven't seen many) is VeggieTales–*Esther: The Girl Who Became Queen*.[4] It downplays perversion as you can imagine, and the humor is fantastic.

2. Choose one character from the book of Esther and begin to meditate on what you learn about that character in Scripture. If you were that particular character, how would you feel as events unfold? What sights and smells might you experience? What would you think? How would you react? Put yourself into the story and consider the details as if you were living them personally.

3. As you read and meditated on the book of Esther, what insights did you gain that you can apply to your life? What promptings did you feel from the Holy Spirit as you studied? Record your thoughts in the space provided below.

Points to Ponder

As we study Esther, we'll find that, unlike Daniel who faithfully held to and practiced Jewish disciplines even during his exile in Babylon, Mordecai and Esther were so assimilated into the Persian culture that they could effectively hide their Jewish heritage. Consider that some modern Christians become so absorbed in our culture they can mask their Christianity. Ponder the level of your own assimilation into our culture. Do you stand out as a "Christ one," or do you blend in with the crowd?

Throughout our time in Esther, consider life in 483 BC compared and contrasted with the present day. What similarities do you see? How are we like the ancient Persians? What types of things have changed through the centuries? How is our civilization different?

CHAPTER 2

It Just So Happened

Please re-read Esther chapter 1 before you continue.

*D*o you believe in coincidence? I don't. In fact, an author I read years ago used the term "God-incidents" from the belief that God orchestrates everything, from the least to the greatest. There are no coincidences, only "God-incidents."

I like that phrasing, don't you?

> *God orchestrates everything,*
> *from the least to the greatest.*

Do Things Happen by Chance?

Let's look into the teachings of Jesus to see if we can catch a glimpse of how he felt about coincidence. In Luke 10:31, in the parable of the Good Samaritan, we read that Jesus said, "A priest *happened* to be going down that road" (italics mine).

At first glance it appears that Jesus conveyed the existence of random activity within the universe, or things that happen by chance. But let's look a little closer.

In this scriptural instance, the word "happened" is translated from the Greek *sygkyria*, a compound word of *sun* (meaning with) and *kyria* (from *kyrios*, meaning supremacy or authority).[1]

Literally, the sentence could read, "and by supreme authority, a priest was going down that road." That doesn't sound like a random occurrence, does it?

Connect this with Proverbs 16:33, which reads, "The lot is cast into the lap, but its every decision is from the Lord."

And with Romans 8:28: "And we know that God causes all things to work together for the good of those who love God, to those who are called according to His purpose" (NASB).

It seems Christ, in Luke 10:31, was making a subtle point about the providence of God and his control over all things.

As the events of Esther unfold, we can say again and again, "It just so happened . . . ," or we can recognize that events are arranged by God's provident hand. I believe (and maybe you do too) that God utilized the desires of King Ahasuerus for his own glory and for the good of his people.

A King's Heart Is in the Lord's Hands

There was a particular desire that held a firm grip on King Ahasuerus: history records that the king's father (King Darius I) led a failed and embarrassing attempt to invade Greece. Ahasuerus developed a passionate hunger for avenging Darius. Many scholars agree that this king-sized desire to conquer Greece was the reason behind the six-month-long banquet described in Esther chapter 1. It was not just an ancient-day pep rally to inspire the leaders of the king's provinces; the king and his military leaders were likely planning their invasion of Greece, which in fact occurred in 480 BC.[2]

The king was extravagant, pouring unlimited wine into golden vessels and displaying intricate adornments believed to have come to Persia as plunder from Solomon's Temple. King Ahasuerus needed to gain favor among his leaders, build their confidence, and show he could uphold promises he had made.

Esther 1:4 reveals his motivation. I see this as a key verse that reveals the heart of the king. It explains the underlying motivation for Ahasuerus throughout the book of Esther was to glorify himself. It reads, "And he displayed the riches of *his* royal glory and the splendor of *his* great majesty" (Est. 1:4 NASB, italics mine).

Part of showing off his splendor, wealth, possessions, and grandeur—in the king's mind at least—was showing off his queen. Vashti was among his most beautiful possessions and at that time in history, women were indeed considered possessions.

Esther 1:11 tells us that the king wanted to show off her beauty to the people and officials—as sort of a one-contestant beauty pageant. But when the king called for Queen Vashti, she refused him. Imagine the embarrassment of a king trying to portray great power and control to a courtyard full of guests. Instead, circumstances revealed that this king couldn't even control a woman. It was a humiliating blow to his ego.

By her disobedience, Queen Vashti's offense was threefold: she was a woman who challenged the authority of a man; she was a wife who disobeyed her husband; and she was a subject who defied the command of the king.

Scripture hints that Vashti may have committed the offense seven separate times. It seems unlikely that the king sent a group of seven eunuchs to deliver a message to the queen. Since each eunuch is named individually in Esther 1:10, it's conceivable that each was sent, one after the other, to deliver her to the banquet. If this were the case, no doubt the king's anger and chagrin escalated with each refusal.

Why Refuse?

The question of the hour is, why did Queen Vashti refuse to come? Scripture doesn't tell us, but there are several schools of thought on the matter:

- A common belief among commentators is that when the king commanded the eunuchs to "bring Queen Vashti before him with her royal crown" (Est. 1:11), he intended that she come wearing *only* the crown and nothing else. If we put ourselves in Vashti's slippers, we can imagine that perhaps her modesty kept her away.

- Queen Vashti gave birth to a son during the same year as the banquet. This son, Artaxerxes, succeeded Ahasuerus on the throne.[3] At the time of the king's famous summons, it's likely that Vashti was a new, hormonal, and exhausted mom who couldn't bring herself to put on a royal show.

- Perhaps she refused due to the indignity of appearing before drunken men.

- Vashti hosted her own feast for the women of the palace, so it's possible that she herself was intoxicated or indisposed.

- Some say she was a prideful and rebellious woman and didn't take orders from anyone.

We'll never know for certain. Regardless of her reason, the king and his advisors saw nothing but rebellion that required swift action. The king was furious. Scripture tells us in Esther 1:12 that his wrath burned, using the Hebrew word *chemah*, which means consuming rage, venom, or poison.[4]

Chemah: consuming rage,
venom, poison

His burning ire required immediate action. Ahasuerus was driven to rescue his reputation, not to mention his ego. The advisors with whom he consulted were motivated to inflate their own importance and ensure the king's continued dependence on them. After drunken consideration the king, following the advice of his royal advisors, legislated that every man should rule and prevail over his own house. Queen Vashti was banished with plans to give her royal position to someone more worthy than she (Est. 1:19, 2:4).

Since we draw our truth from Scripture, we'll never know why Vashti didn't answer the king's page. Whether or not we agree with her actions or the king's response, the stage was set for God to appoint a new queen. Chance and coincidence had little to do with the matter at all. In the citadel of Susa and every province of Persia, the Lord was about to show his might in a profound yet deafeningly silent manner.

> *The Lord was about to show his might in a profound yet deafeningly silent manner.*

From Persia to Present Day

Years ago, I remember a friend exclaiming, "Wow, that's providence!" I recall the question bouncing through my mind, "What does that mean?" By her context, I could tell it was a statement that pertained to God, but I didn't understand its connotation. Before I could ask, our conversation took a different turn and I made a mental note to look it up later.

As Christians, we often speak "Christianese," don't we? We use terms and phrases that seem common to us, but those outside church circles rarely understand our words. Words like providence, sanctification, and propitiation come to mind—as well as substitutionary atonement and even the ideas of surrender, holiness, grace, and mercy.

So before I marvel at how God reveals his providence and his sovereignty, let's take a look at what these terms mean.

Providence

The *Dictionary of Bible Themes* defines "providence" as "the continuing and often unseen activity of God in sustaining his universe, providing for the needs of every creature, and preparing for the completion of his eternal purposes."[5]

More simply stated, the *Lexham Bible Dictionary* defines "providence" as "God's plan and interaction with his creation."[6]

My favorite description is from Dr. Augustus Hopkins Strong who says, "Providence is God's attention concentrated everywhere."[7]

What a beautiful thought. Have you ever considered that we capture God's attention? We are the apple of his eye (Ps. 17:8 NASB), and his thoughts toward us are of vast number (Ps. 139:17). Not only does he give us his attention; also he concentrates it upon every part of our lives. There is nothing—not one thing—that escapes his watchful care.

Ponder on the idea that he inscribed us in the palm of his hands (Isa. 49:16). I once heard one of my favorite Bible teachers share that every single thing that God allows in our lives must be filtered through his loving fingers. If we are nestled, protected, and sheltered within the palm of God's hand, nothing can get to us without his focused gaze that takes notice. God "works out everything in agreement with the decision of His will" (Eph. 1:11).

Every single thing that God allows in our lives must be filtered through his loving fingers.

Sovereignty

Sovereignty is a characteristic of God that pairs with providence. Consider that God's providence is his direct involvement in every aspect of our lives. Couple that with his sovereignty, which means that God possesses all power and is the ruler of all things (see Ps. 135:6 and Dan. 4:35–36).[8]

We can arrive at an understanding that God interacts with, sees, and controls all things in our lives.

Since we know that God is love and his love is unconditional (Deut. 7:6–8 and Rom. 5:8) . . .

Since we know that Christ gave himself up for us as an act of purifying redemption to make us his own possession (Titus 2:14) . . .

And since we know that God's grace was granted us in Christ Jesus from all eternity (2 Tim. 1:9) . . .

We can rest assured that he works all things together for our good. True, he sometimes allows events and circumstances that are unpleasant and downright painful. Even when we're on a twisted and seemingly treacherous path, we can trust God fearlessly, for he works according to his character, care, and constant love. His aim is always his glory and our good, and God never misses his aim.

> *We can trust God fearlessly, for he works according to his character, care, and constant love.*

A friend once shared a meme on Facebook that delineated the following six reasons to trust the Lord:[9]

1. He knows you by name (Isa. 43:1).

2. He thinks about you (Ps. 139:17).

3. He will fight for you (Ex. 14:14).

4. He is your refuge (Ps. 62:6–8).

5. He has a plan for you (Jer. 29:11).

6. He is always with you (Matt. 28:20).

We know that through God's providence and sovereignty we are protected, even when it feels as if the walls are crumbling around us. How does this knowledge help you find peace in the midst of your pending divorce, the next round of chemotherapy, or the news of your husband's job loss? How does it encourage your heart to know that the God of love is perfectly in control of all things? Does it help you stay in the fight against your daily struggle with addiction or move you deeper into the spiritual battle against your daughter's drug use? Can you use this understanding to keep your eyes on the unseen and watch the horizon for a forthcoming victory in your current circumstance?

I pray it does, and I've asked the Lord to help us all walk in the assurance of our faith.

Hang in there, dear one. Your celebration is coming because God is for you. And if he is for you, what can stand against you? (Rom. 8:31).

With the vocabulary defined, it becomes obvious that God's sovereignty and providence, even without his visible interaction, are evident throughout the book of Esther.

Digging Deeper

1. Re-read Esther chapter 1 and identify what you see as the king's weaknesses. List them here:

2. What biblical characters can you name who have exhibited pride and/or anger?

3. In the space below, write out three or more Bible verses that provide instruction or advice on pride and/or anger. (Google is often a good resource to find topical Bible verses. Other helpful Internet tools: biblegateway.com, blueletterbible.org, or biblestudytools.com. Or, you can also use a concordance for help.)

4. What, if anything, do you learn about Queen Vashti in Esther chapter 1?

5. Why do you suppose Queen Vashti refused to obey the king? Can you think of reasons other than those provided?

6. If you were Queen Vashti, how would you have responded to the king's command? Read Romans 13:1–7. Does this change your answer? Explain.

7. It was common for kings to consult men "who knew the times." (See Est. 1:13 and 1 Chron. 12:32). According to Daniel 2:2, what were the professions of these advisors?

What is the Lord's instruction pertaining to mediums and sorcery in Leviticus 19:31 and Exodus 22:18?

8. Contrast the practices of men who "knew the times" with Paul's teaching in Ephesians 5:17. How would one come to know the will of the Lord?

9. Do you feel that the king or his advisors exaggerated the problem of Queen Vashti's disobedience? Why or why not?

10. Do you see evidence in Scripture that the king's advisors manipulated him through their advice? Explain your answer.

11. How does the king's edict (Est. 1:20–22) comply with God's command in Colossians 3:18 and Ephesians 5:22–27?

Do you see any conflict between the edict and these references? Explain.

Do you feel that the king's edict honored the letter of God's New Testament command but not the spirit (or heart) of the command in Colossians 3:18 and Ephesians 5:22–27?

12. As you read and meditated on Scripture, what insights did you gain that you can apply to your life? What promptings did you feel from the Holy Spirit as you studied?

Points to Ponder

Would you describe the events in the book of Esther as coincidence and happenstance? Or maybe you'd consider them a demonstration of God's sovereignty and providence. How might you debate your position with a trusted friend?

I've read that the custom in ancient Persia allowed mixed company at banquets (men and women attending together). Why do you suppose that Queen Vashti held a separate banquet for the women? Does Esther 1:9 help us understand more about the events that unfolded? How so?

How does Christ treat his bride (the church) as we submit to him? In other words, how does the Bridegroom, Christ, lovingly care for his bride? How does that differ from King Ahasuerus's actions?

What does it mean to submit to our husbands as is fitting to the Lord (Col. 3:18)?

CHAPTER 3

Crowned and Snubbed

Please re-read Esther chapter 2 before you continue.

M ost English Bible translations begin chapter 2 of
Esther with the words "Some time later" or
"After these things." While the phrase is
nondescript, it seems several years have ticked away between
chapter 1 and chapter 2.

After What Things?

Look back to Esther 1:3. The king's six-month banquet
took place during the third year of his reign, in 483 BC. Esther 2:16
tells us that Esther was taken to the king's palace four years later,
in the seventh year of his reign, in 479 BC.

Some of us learned in history courses that between 483
BC and 479 BC, the span of time now noted between the banquet
and Esther's coronation, King Ahasuerus led an ambitious yet ill-
fated military campaign against Greece. We can easily imagine
that he returned home humiliated, mentally defeated, and weary.

This might be a time when a king would long to return to
the arms of his wife, but this king no longer had a wife. He had
banished his queen. When he returned home from the war, the
king's anger against Vashti subsided and he "remembered" her

(Est. 2:1). He allowed himself to bring her to mind, to reconsider what she'd done, and what was decided against her.

The language in Esther 2:1 suggests that the king refused to accept personal responsibility for her banishment but instead placed the blame on his advisors. Sadly, we'll see that the experience with Vashti didn't deter him from acting on poor counsel in the future.

What's So Great about a Wife?

As the king remembered Vashti, he was troubled and missed her. He had concubines, plenty of them, but missed a wife who offered a deeper level of trust, companionship, and intimacy than women from his harem. His servants and attendants noticed the king's longing and immediately moved into action. They set plans to assemble a new harem for their ruler. From this fresh collection of young, beautiful virgins, the king would choose a new queen.

After they were gathered and beautified, each young virgin auditioned for the role of queen by spending the night in the king's chambers. Even to a king, such a chain of lovers could become tiresome. In King Ahasuerus's longing for a wife, it's possible that he grew discouraged in his quest to replace Vashti. None of the young ladies completely satisfied him—that is, until Esther appeared.

The Jewess who would become queen stood out from the rest of the women. She was different, and the Word tells us that she gained the favor of everyone who met her. This included men and women alike—from servants to sister contestants for the crown. Everyone Esther met showed her grace and good will. They genuinely liked her. Some, including Hegai who was in charge of the beauty queens, even hoped she would "win" and provided preferential treatment.

When Esther entered the king's chambers that night, she did more than satisfy his sexual cravings; I believe she connected with his mind and heart. Esther 2:17 tells us that the king loved her more than all the virgins. The Hebrew word translated "love" in this instance is *'ahab*, which denotes human affection toward a person or a thing. It includes appetite or hunger toward its object, and depicts sexual love as well as friendship.[1]

The king quickly chose Esther as his new wife—not merely for her outward looks but for her inner beauty.

Listen to what God's Word says about true beauty in 1 Peter 3:4: "Instead, it should consist of what is inside the heart with the imperishable quality of a gentle and quiet spirit, which is very valuable in God's eyes."

It is interesting that in the context of this description of beauty, Peter is specifically addressing wives. This type of unfading beauty was obviously of great worth to the king of Persia as it is to Jesus, the King of kings.

Not only did King Ahasuerus give Esther his love; he also gave her kindness. Her gentleness seemed to calm his intensity, and by yielding to his authority, she received a good deal of leniency that we'll see throughout the book.

Mordecai Saves the King

After Esther was crowned, and from his position at the king's gate, Mordecai, Esther's uncle, overheard two of his coworkers discuss a plot to kill King Ahasuerus. He didn't take the news to the king's prime minister. He delivered it to Esther, the queen, who relayed it to the king in Mordecai's name.

After an investigation confirmed the story, the two men were hanged on the gallows. A hanging in Persia likely meant gruesome impalement on a pole. Persians were not known for their mercy toward criminals, and it's believed that this society may have later established the practice of crucifixion. They took their capital punishment quite seriously and carried it out immediately.

These events and the averted plot to kill the king were recorded in the historical records of Susa (Est. 2:23). Of noteworthy absence, however, was a reward for Mordecai. Traditional recognition for one who saved a king's life may have included forgiveness of all future taxes owed. By the king's choosing, the man might have been freed from the requirement to bow before nobility. Hold on to this nugget. It will become important in later chapters.

From Persia to Present Day

Perhaps you understand the emotions that Mordecai might have felt about the lack of gratitude expressed to him.

While I don't believe for a moment that he disclosed the plot on the king's life to achieve personal gain, surely he noticed that the king didn't even say thank you. Have you ever experienced such a surprising disappointment after going out of your way to walk in uprightness?

We can't leap to a conclusion that reporting the assassination plot was an easy decision for Mordecai. While he may not have hesitated in doing the right thing, it's worthy of notice that the king wasn't a nice man.

Esther's uncle may have agreed with the grievances his two coworkers had against their liege. Mordecai could have kept quiet and maintained unity within the ranks. He could have gone about his business, kept his nose to the grindstone, and convinced himself that he must not have overheard the conversation correctly. Instead, he acted with integrity and morality. He took the hard road and protected his king.

Is it human nature that would have led Mordecai to imagine and hope for gratitude from the king? Would it have been reasonable for Mordecai to expect the king to be pleased and even humbled by his action? Mordecai saved his life, for

40

goodness' sake! A thank you note would have gone a long way in Mordecai's mind.

> *Mordecai acted with integrity*
> *and morality.*

Imagine if Susa had mail carriers. Mordecai might have asked day after day if a note from the king had arrived. Or maybe he would have secretly hoped to receive an interview and a plaque from his local news channel recognizing him as an "Everyday Hero." But there was no such pomp. No such circumstance.

Our minds can easily twist into knots of entitlement, can't they? It's not often easy to move against the mainstream to do what is upright and virtuous. When we make the effort, it feels reasonable to expect someone of prominence to recognize our efforts. Or show some gratitude. When the appreciation doesn't come, it's natural to feel disappointed.

But we serve a God who doesn't miss a single detail. He sees everything that we think, say, and do. When our righteous acts go unnoticed by our society, when we somehow fly under the radar, we know that the God of the universe sees the whole scene from start to finish. Our reward is coming—either in this lifetime or the next—and we can trust that our Father in heaven will not let it go without notice. Trusting that he sees brings us peace so that we can let go of our tendency to strive for the approval of others. God's approval is enough, and he will show his pleasure in due time.

> *When we somehow fly under the*
> *radar, we know that the God of the*
> *universe saw the whole scene from*
> *start to finish.*

Let's trust God to work out all of the details in our own lives.

Soon, we'll see exactly how the king handles Mordecai's recognition—and it is glorious. Just you wait and see. For now, let's dig a little deeper.

Digging Deeper

1. First introductions in Scripture are important and usually provide significant details. Re-read Esther chapter 2 and list everything you learn about Mordecai and Esther.

Mordecai

Esther

What evidence do you see in Esther 2 that Esther possessed the following characteristics? (Provide scriptural references).

- She was lovely.

- She had a difficult past.

- She was teachable.

- She showed humility.

- She showed grace and charm (and therefore found favor).

- She showed restraint and self-control.

- She showed respect for authority.

- She showed bravery.

2. Which of Esther's characteristics do you believe are pleasing to Christ? Which of these characteristics would you most like to emulate

3. Read Esther 2:8 below:

> "So it came about when the command and decree of the king were heard and many young ladies were gathered to the citadel of Susa into the custody of Hegai, that Esther was taken to the king's palace into the custody of Hegai, who was in charge of the women" (NASB).

Does it seem that the young virgins went to the palace voluntarily? Explain your answer.

4. How might the families of these young women have responded to the command and decree of the king? Would they have had a favorable reaction? Why or why not?

5. What do you see in Esther 2:10–11 that indicates how Mordecai felt about Esther in the palace? How did he check on her?

6. Why do you think that Esther's immediate genealogy was listed in Esther 2:15? (The following question may provide a clue.)

7. The name Abihail (Esther's father) means "father of strength, bravery."[2] Do you think that Esther needed strength and bravery to enter the king's chambers? Explain.

8. What evidence do you see of God's hand in Esther 2?

9. What evidence do you see that God uses ordinary people? How were each of these characters used by God?

   • Mordecai

   • Esther

- Hegai

- Abihail

(I'll offer my speculation: since his name means bravery, perhaps Abihail had the opportunity to model bravery for Esther before his death. That bravery might have been used by God to spur Esther to great action, which ultimately saved the Jews in Persia.)

10. How do you believe that God might want to use you? What promptings do you feel to use your spiritual gifts and pursue his calling in your life?

11. Esther, a young orphan raised by her cousin, miraculously found herself in a royal position in the palace. She was an ordinary woman who encountered extraordinary circumstances that prepared her for God's intended purpose. Reading her story can make us long for a miraculous story of our own. Take some time to consider whether you're waiting for an extraordinary circumstance (maybe waiting for your "big break") before pursuing the call that God has placed on your life. Record your thoughts below.

12. One of the overarching themes of this study is to watch for God in the ordinary moments of life. Big breaks and extraordinary circumstances are the exception rather than the norm, and if we allow ourselves to sit idle and wait for the miraculous, we often miss subtle opportunities that the Lord provides. Listen to the opening line of Psalm 37:34 that instructs us in how we should wait: "Wait for the Lord *and keep His way*" (italics mine).

   List a few ways that you can actively keep God's way while you wait. What steps can you take, day by day, to actively prepare for your calling and watch with expectation for God? (See Ps. 130:5.)

13. As you read and meditated on Scripture, what insights did you gain that you can apply to your life? What promptings did you feel from the Holy Spirit as you studied?

Points to Ponder

When the young virgins were taken to the palace, life as they knew it was essentially over. Any dreams they had of marriage and raising a family were forfeited. Many (if not all) of them could expect to lose their virginity to a man who would not show the slightest bit of affection and may never call for them again.

Each virgin had a slim chance at being chosen as queen, but for the vast majority, their futures would feel more like widowhood without ever having known love. Palace life was sure to offer plush and luxurious living conditions, but it was essentially a prison.

The sexual environment in Persia was not only perverse, it was oppressive, and not just to women. Hundreds of young men were also captured each year and made eunuchs to serve in the palace.

If Persian men and women were anything like those in our current culture, many found their identity in their given roles. Whether she followed God or not, a woman in this era identified her purpose through bearing children and bringing honor to a husband. For those robbed of this experience, it would have been easy to succumb to feelings of desperation, or shame, or hopelessness.

In what do you place your personal identity? In your friendships? In your role as a daughter, or wife, or mother? As a student, or homemaker, or professional? In your creativity, logic, or other gifts and talents?

Every role that we accept in life has a beginning and an end. Only one thing lasts forever, and that is our relationship with Jesus Christ. As his followers we are to find our identity in him and in what his Word says about us.

To what Scriptures do you cling when you're tempted to succumb to self-condemnation? How do you remind yourself that you are a child of the King, holy and blameless in his sight?

(To view the Scriptures that I commonly use, visit http://www.strengthenedbytheword.com/ and click on the "Freebies" tab. I have them gathered together in what I call my "Emergency Scripture & Quote Cards.")

CHAPTER 4

A Picture of Evil

Please re-read Esther chapter 3 before you continue.

*I*n the closing lines of Esther chapter 2, Mordecai rescued King Ahasuerus from a plot against his life. Remember, the king overlooked Mordecai, never recognizing him for his act of bravery. It was a common practice to esteem such a hero with forgiveness of taxes or eliminating the requirement that he bow before nobility. In Ahasuerus's day a worthy hero might have received recognition as an honorary noble. Instead, as we see in the opening verses of Esther chapter 3, the king promoted another man, Haman, and commanded the people to bow and pay homage to his new prime minister.

What If?

Will you play a game with me? Let's try one of my daughter's favorite brainteasers and ask, "What if . . . ?"

What if . . . Mordecai had received timely commendation?

What if . . . Mordecai was never required to pay homage to Haman? What then?

If that were the case, history and the events of Esther would have taken an entirely different turn. This was a pivotal moment in Persia, to be sure.

Through the king's lack of attention to this one detail, through his failure to acknowledge Mordecai, we see another glorious ripple in history, ordained by God and orchestrated by his invisible hand.

Let's revisit Proverbs 21:1: "A king's heart is like streams of water in the Lord's hand: He directs it wherever He chooses."

We see scriptural evidence that it is the Lord who moves kings. Consider the following instances:

- Exodus 9:12 when the Lord hardened Pharaoh's heart;

- Ezra 1:1 when the Lord stirred up the spirit of Cyrus, king of Persia;

- and our current place in Esther when the Lord ordained that Ahasuerus would overlook an important detail about Mordecai.

Fear not! Our beloved Mordecai will receive his just reward. In his commentary on Ruth and Esther, Warren Wiersbe beautifully states, "The Lord will not forsake the righteous nor leave their deeds unrewarded."[1] We see this as truth throughout Scripture, including Mordecai's predicament.

Wrapped in Rage

In the meantime, Mordecai and the entire royal staff were required to bow before nobility. But Mordecai refused.

When his coworkers asked him why he disobeyed, Mordecai admitted his Jewish heritage, which prevented him from bowing or paying homage to Haman. His friends (I'm using that term lightly) begged him daily to follow the king's command, but Mordecai would not. And so, like children on a playground, they tattled.

Haman's reaction was fierce. We again see the use of the Hebrew transliteration *chemah* (used earlier to describe the king's anger when Vashti disobeyed). This time it was Haman who expressed *chemah*—or a level of rage that is consuming and venomous.[2] Haman's fury was so intense, so poisonous, it didn't stop at Mordecai alone. It was as if Haman loaded a nuclear-tipped arrowhead into his bow and pointed it at Mordecai fully knowing the degree of carnage to come.

Haman's intent was to destroy all the Jews. The word translated as "destroy" in Esther 3:6 is the Hebrew *shamad*. It means to exterminate.[3] We use that term when we rid our homes of insect infestations. When we call an exterminator, we don't want the bugs mostly gone; we want them *shamad*. It means to annihilate, to devastate. Haman meant business. He was out to rid the world, beginning with his corner of it, of an entire race of people.

> *When we call an exterminator, we don't want the bugs mostly gone; we want them* shamad.

Haman didn't act with rash impulse. He plotted carefully. His first stop was consultation with diviners who cast lots to determine a date for destruction. Literally, they calendared the annihilation of the Jews.

Lots (or *Pur*) were cubes made of clay and inscribed with prayers. The clay stones were shaken in a jar or the fold of a garment until one fell out.[4] By casting lots, Haman received what he believed was divine approval of his plan and an inspired date: the thirteenth day of Adar, which was nearly a full year into the future.

Next, Haman approached King Ahasuerus. The king nodded in ready agreement to the plan "to destroy, to kill and to annihilate all the Jews, both young and old, women and children, in one day . . . and to seize their possessions as plunder" (Est. 3:13

NASB). He refused a remarkable bribe from Haman and elected instead to replenish the royal treasuries, surely diminished by the recent war, with plunder.

The king and Haman then sat down to toast their impressive leadership, but the entire city was in confusion. A command, which surely seemed to come from out of nowhere, had just been issued to the officials and people of Persia. The command hit home: neighbors, friends, business owners, and even royal officials who were Jews would soon experience utter destruction and loss of life.

The people of Persia were likely bewildered and overcome, wondering, "Why? What have we done to bring about such hatred?"

From Persia to Present Day

An anger as profound as Haman's was most certainly spurred on by something greater than one man's refusal to pay homage. In our Digging Deeper section, we'll spend some time researching the relationship between the forefathers of Mordecai and those of Haman. We'll gather the history that spawned a level of hatred in Haman that was deep enough to crave annihilation.

Spoiler alert: we will see that the generational hatred initially borne by Haman's and Mordecai's ancestors was perpetuated by one king's partial obedience to the Lord's command.

It is said that partial obedience is disobedience. Unless we fully obey what the Lord directs us to do, we are walking in disobedience. And that robs us of blessing. Consider the following Scriptures:

- Luke 11:28—Jesus said, "Even more, those who hear the word of God and keep it are blessed!" (To "keep" God's word means to do it or put it into action.)

52

- John 14:15—Jesus said, "If you love Me, you will keep My commands."

- Romans 6:16—"Don't you know that if you offer yourselves to someone as obedient slaves, you are slaves of that one you obey – either of sin leading to death or of obedience leading to righteousness?"

- Isaiah 1:19—"If you are willing and obedient, you will eat the good things of the land."

I can remember the first time I specifically "heard" the Lord tell me to do something. I didn't hear it with my ears; rather, I felt the direction deep in my spirit while listening to a speaker at a women's tea. However, the words didn't come from the speaker; they came from the Holy Spirit.

Later, I discovered that the instruction was consistent with a command in Scripture (see James 5:16). Through the power of his Spirit, the Lord instructed me to confess something exceedingly painful to a family member.

I didn't want to do it, and I could justify my unwillingness in a thousand ways. My confession would hurt others. I believed it would disrupt peace and unity in our family. Such confessions when there seemed no apparent need are just not done. This was early in my Christian walk, and my way of thinking was evidence of my spiritual immaturity at the time.

I spent close to a year arguing with the Lord. His instruction plagued me. It consumed my thoughts, and very few moments went by without his words resonating in my spirit. I lost sleep. I had trouble eating. The peace I thought I had was stripped away and replaced with utter turmoil. I vividly remember looking in the mirror one day and saying aloud, "You need to have yourself committed. God doesn't talk to people, and you are NOT going to do this."

In my heart of hearts, I knew that if I confessed this thing, my family life would never look the same. I would lose my husband whom I dearly loved. He would surely fight for custody of our very young kids, and I would lose them too. But I could no longer stand the torment.

Throughout my year of disobedience, the Lord continued to show me who he is. I seemed to hear the message repeatedly that he is trustworthy. That his plans never fail. That he is for me. That he blesses those who are obedient to him. One day I realized I could no longer disobey. I came to the realization that I had truly received real-life, very personal instruction from the Lord.

I laid aside my self-sufficiency and pride. I decided to surrender to the Lord of the universe and follow his lead. I took a deep breath and placed my trust in him, waiting to see what would come of it. I had learned over those twelve months that God loved my family and saw our every need. He knew my kids needed their mommy. He knew the depth of love I had for my man. I didn't want our family to disintegrate, and I knew the Lord didn't want to see that either.

So I stepped out in faith. I took off my mask and I told the truth. At the very instant I opened my mouth to DO what the Lord instructed me to do, I was flooded with peace and reassurance. I knew the journey wouldn't be easy, but I would receive his blessing because I was honoring God instead of protecting my reputation. After a long battle, I chose trust over disbelief and God proved faithful.

I didn't lose my marriage. We off-roaded through some crater-sized potholes and nearly went off of a few cliffs, but we made it. And our love and loyalty to one another are deeper than ever. Our immediate family is not perfect—we never have been—but we are whole, happy, and blessed.

After investigating the history of the Agagites, the ancestors of Haman, and the level of hatred that carried through generations of people (we'll study this together in the Digging Deeper section), I'm exceedingly grateful that the Holy Spirit chased after me so hard. I can't imagine the pain of realizing that my disobedience might have caused perpetual bitterness to take root in the lives of my children and grandchildren. Instead, I recognize God's daily protection over my kids. It makes this momma's heart want to sing in unending praise.

All these decades later, this is still the biggest leap of faith I have ever taken. Since then, even the monumental steps of obedience somehow seem easy, even when things look impossible. It's because I know the Lord is with me and I trust that he'll take on all of the heavy lifting.

When we follow hard after him, he lavishes his blessings upon us. I heard once that when the Lord lavishes, it's as if we place our empty cups beneath Niagara Falls. He pours out his provision with the power and abundance of that great waterfall. I believe it.

If you are wrestling with the Lord over a particular matter, with all my heart I encourage you to bathe the situation in prayer and walk in obedience. First, confirm that the instruction that you perceive is consistent with God's Word. The Holy Spirit will never lead you in ways that are contrary to the Bible. If what you discern is in opposition to the Scriptures, it's not from God. It's from the Enemy. However, if what you discern is confirmed through God's Word, don't delay in acting.

Immediate obedience is always best, but if a delay is inevitable, I suggest you confide in a trusted spiritual mentor. Choose someone who is intimate with the Bible and knows it well. Choose someone who demonstrates obedience in her own life and seek her counsel. Then act. Please don't delay. Trust and obey.

Digging Deeper

1. Re-read Esther 3:1–15. Haman was an Agagite (Est. 3:1), likely a descendant of King Agag who ruled the Amalekites (1 Sam. 15:8). Let's retrace the history of Israel and the Amalekites. Read Exodus 17:8–16 (one of my favorite Bible passages for its profound demonstration of the power of intercession, but

we'll save that discussion for another time). Joshua led Israel in a battle against Amalek at Rephidim.

What does Exodus 17:14-16 tell us about what would come of the Amalekites?

2. Read Deuteronomy 25:17–18.

   • What did the Amalekites do to the Israelites as they came out of Egypt?

   • Think of the Israelites during the exodus. What sort of people might have been the exhausted "stragglers" in the rear?

3. Read 1 Samuel chapter 15.

   • What specific instructions did the Lord give to King Saul in verse 3?

   • What did King Saul actually do, according to verses 8 and 9?

   • What reason did King Saul give for his response, as described in verses 15, 20, and 21?

   • In verse 18, what words are used to describe the destruction of the Amalekites?

- What similarities do you see in Esther 3?

- How did Samuel reply to King Saul's defensive answer in verses 22 and 23?

- What were the consequences of King Saul's disobedience (1 Sam. 15:26–28)?

- What action did Samuel take, according to verse 33?

- What unresolved grudge-holding do you see in your own family lines?

- When pain turns to anger, how do we prevent anger from turning into meanness that escalates beyond reason? Practically, how can we release generational anger?

- What steps might the Lord be prompting you to take in a relationship needing reconciliation? How will you respond to that prompting?

4. Read Proverbs 6:16–19 and list the seven things that are an abomination to the Lord:

1.

2.

3.

4.

5.

6.

7.

- Place a checkmark next to any traits from the list above that you see in Haman. Do you believe that referring to Haman as an evil man is accurate?

5. As you read and meditated on Scripture, what insights did you gain that you can apply to your life? What promptings did you feel from the Holy Spirit as you studied?

Points to Ponder

Esther 3 contains fifteen short verses jam-packed with historical inference. I think of Donkey, the character in the movie *Shrek*, and his reference to onions. They have a lot of layers. So does Esther 3!

The Lord is not one to waste words, so when he speaks through Scripture, we can expect that he provides information for specific application. I encourage you to seek and heed the prompting of the Holy Spirit as we consider another hidden nugget regarding the many dates mentioned in Esther 3, which may not mean much to us at first glance. It's hard to think through dates on a foreign calendar. But even if we don't know Nisan from Adar, we can put the puzzle together here.

*Even if we don't know Nisan
from Adar, we can put
the puzzle together.*

Re-read Esther 3:12 below:

"Then the king's scribes were summoned *on the thirteenth day of the first month*, and it was written just as Haman commanded to the king's satraps, to the governors who were over each province and to the princes of each people, each province according to its script, each people according to its language, being written in the name of King Ahasuerus and sealed with the king's signet ring" (NASB, Italics mine).

Now read Leviticus 23:4–5, which details the date ordained for Passover. Do you see the connection between the date mentioned here and the date shown above in Esther 3:12?

The edict to destroy God's people was written on the thirteenth day of Nisan, the first month. It's not a stretch to suppose that actual distribution of the order began on the fourteenth day.

Did you catch it?

In the very moments that the Jews prepared and celebrated Passover, King Ahasuerus's order to destroy their people was delivered among the provinces. On that very evening, in accordance with established Jewish tradition, fathers would retell the story of the Israelites' deliverance from Egypt. Every Jewish family would hear of God's sovereignty over the hand of an oppressive national leader.

For the Jews, this wasn't a story about events that happened to "someone else." These events unfolded in the lives of their own flesh and blood—prior generations that were known and identified. The dramatic stories were real, personal, and passed down as eyewitness accounts from those in their own family trees.

There's no doubt that while God's hand seemed absent, this timing was not coincidental. His great love and mercy afforded his people a glance at a mighty memorial stone. Through efficient use of the kingdom calendar and ordained tradition, God silently whispered, "Remember, I am with you. I am for you. You are mine." Beloved friend, he says that you and me, too.

> *"Remember, I am with you. I am for you. You are mine."*

We've had a healthy amount of Bible reading in this section of our homework. If you're up for a little more, take time to thumb through the book of Exodus and reacquaint yourself with the bondage and oppression that the Israelites experienced in Egypt. Look again at the ten plagues inflicted upon the Egyptians and how the Lord provided for deliverance of the nation. Then revisit your favorite gospel account of the New Testament celebration of Passover in the upper room and the Lamb who was slain at the crucifixion.

CHAPTER 5

Counting the Cost

Please re-read Esther chapter 4 before you continue.

*I*n Persia, the decree of a king could not be overturned. Not even by a king. This is a difficult concept to understand, especially in our current US political structure, which allows for a new leader every four years and in which our legislative branch of government makes laws only to revise or repeal them later. It seems logical that if a king issued a decree, he could revoke it. That was not the case in Persia. Once sealed by the royal ring, an order was irrevocable (see Dan. 6:8).

> *Once sealed by the royal ring, an order was irrevocable.*

When the king's decree was issued in Esther 3, Mordecai was one of the first to receive the news of the coming destruction of Jews scattered throughout the Persian Empire. Those ordered to be exterminated were Mordecai's people—approximately fifteen million of them living across the 127 provinces from India to Ethiopia. Of worthy note is the inclusion of Jerusalem in the king's region of reign.

Since Mordecai lived in Susa and held an official position at the king's gate, he didn't merely hear the news or read a posted copy. He held in his hand "a copy of the written decree issued in Susa" (Est. 4:8). This struck his heart and he wailed loudly and bitterly, dressed in sackcloth and ashes.

Because of his grieving, Mordecai could not enter the king's gate, for a king in Persia was sheltered from sorrow and misery. Esther sent garments to clothe Mordecai, perhaps so that he could come to speak with her inside the gate—or perhaps because through her time in the palace, she too had become consumed with appearances. Mordecai was causing a scene, and Esther may have wanted to smooth over the way things looked. Whatever her reason, Mordecai refused Esther's attempts to comfort and assist him.

Rabbinical teachings explain that to accept comfort is equivalent to giving up hope. For example, Jacob refused comfort in order to maintain hope that his son Joseph was still alive (Gen. 37:34–35). Consider family members of a missing person who resist grieving because of the hope of rescue. "In such cases, grief lacks closure. To refuse to be comforted is to refuse to give up hope."[1]

In spite of the visible evidence, Mordecai chose not to accept what seemed inevitable and instead kept his eyes on the unseen. He had "something else to set against it—a faith, a trust, an unbreakable hope that proved stronger" than circumstance.[2] And so Mordecai mourned loudly in the public square. He attracted the attention of his adopted daughter, Queen Esther, who sent her attendant, Hathach, to learn more. Using their go-between, Mordecai implored Esther to plead with the king for the lives of her people.

Hathach's Service

Mordecai specifically used the phrase "her people." Again, Mordecai let the cat out of the bag, this time revealing Esther's heritage to Hathach, her servant. Hathach's reaction is not recorded, despite the fact that Esther's Jewish heritage was a secret she had kept for five years. Was Hathach himself a Jew?

It's possible. Like Daniel and others in Babylon, Jewish exiles were often placed into royal service. We can't be sure, but we see that Hathach acted with discretion and relayed the message with accuracy. Did he realize the importance of his role?

At Mordecai's request that Esther approach the king, the queen responded, "All the royal officials and the people of the royal provinces know that one law applies to every man or woman who approaches the king in the inner courtyard and who has not been summoned—the death penalty" (Est. 4:11).

Perhaps Hathach was among those who advised against interrupting the king. It's likely Esther's winsomeness had won him over. I doubt he cared to imagine her sentenced to death and assumed that silence would protect her life. Esther surely made the same assumption.

Mordecai's Three Points of Wisdom

Mordecai soon put an end to that short-lived fantasy with the reminder that the decree was for the destruction of all Jews. Her marriage to King Ahasuerus would not protect Esther's life. This is the first of three points that Mordecai stressed through the messenger.

Her marriage to King Ahasuerus would not protect Esther's life.

Secondly, Mordecai emphasized that deliverance would come with or without Esther. God would accomplish his purpose even if his servants refused to obey his will. Like Esther, we have a choice to make: walk in obedience and trust that the Lord will work in and through us to accomplish his divine purposes or refuse to get involved and miss the blessings that await us.

> *Deliverance would come with or*
> *without Esther.*

The Bible demonstrates that if we choose disobedience, the Lord will:

- Find another servant to do the job. When John Mark left the mission field, the Lord raised up Silas and Timothy and worked mightily through them (Acts 13:13, 15:36–41, 16:1–3).

- Discipline us until we surrender. When Jonah ran from his assignment, the Lord pursued him until he obeyed. (Refer to the book of Jonah to refresh your memory.)

Finally, Mordecai reminded Esther that her position in the palace was no accident. The implication is strong that the Lord appointed her as queen "for such a time as this" (Est. 4:14). God has divine purposes whether he works through the kings of nations or in the hearts of his people. Nothing is outside of his provident domain.

> *The Lord appointed her as queen*
> *"for such a time as this."*

Esther listened. She heard. Mordecai captured her heart, and she decided to take action, calling for a fast among her people (Est. 4:16).

From Persia to Present Day

My mom despises driving. She always has.

This is a foreign idea to me. There's not much I love more than a road trip, losing myself in loud music, singing my heart out (to the dismay of those in the car with me), while watching the dotted highway lines tick by. I do some of my best thinking while driving. I certainly do some of my best singing from behind a steering wheel; don't you? It's even better than in the shower.

The day I turned sixteen and received my driver's license, my mom handed me her keys and let me be her chauffeur until I moved away to college. There was tremendous freedom and joy in that old 1978 Pontiac Grand Am, but there was one huge point of frustration: the car had no stereo. None.

It's the only car I've ever seen without a sound system of any sort. In the dashboard, where a radio and maybe even a cassette tape player would normally be, was a piece of PVC that matched the rest of the car's interior. It was like a surgical wound that had healed over without a scar.

Can you envision a sixteen-year-old girl driving around in a car with her girlfriends, listening to . . . nothing? I couldn't either. So I pulled my boom box out of my bedroom, loaded it with batteries, and took it on the road. Before long the retractable antenna snapped off and the portable radio had considerable trouble tuning into our local radio stations. Sometimes if I held the remaining antenna nub with my right hand while I drove with my left, I could hear an entire song. In every instance that a 1980s hit came through the speakers with clarity, it made me want to stop on the side of the road to have a good long listen.

There's a point to this story that ties back to Queen Esther. Really. And it's something I've recently learned.

When I practice the spiritual discipline of a fast, it helps me tune into the Holy Spirit like those moments when an FM station boomed with clarity through my makeshift car stereo. I know, that surely sounds strange, so please let me explain.

To Fast or Not to Fast

For years I've had an intense curiosity about fasting. I tried it a few times, to a degree that I consider unsuccessful. One time

I fasted and prayed through lunch. When I felt I had prayed to a point of completion, I "negotiated" with God and was eating a sandwich by 2:00 p.m. Most of the other times when I tried to abstain from food, I considered how much weight I might lose. It was clear my heart was far from the right place to practice the spiritual discipline. My desires and intent were focused on self and were anything but holy or righteous.

Little by little and over many years, I developed a deeper understanding about what a fast is, how one works, and the reasons behind fasting. And as I practiced and developed the discipline, the benefits became obvious. I now consider fasting one of the most life-changing spiritual disciplines I am blessed to experience.

I'll keep things very simple here and share a few of the highlights that I've learned and some of the blessings that I've seen.

Jesus provided instruction for fasting in Matthew 6:16-18. He started by setting the expectation saying "Whenever you fast . . ." Note he did not say *if* you fast, but he emphasized *when*. Fasting is expected, just as prayer and giving, as mentioned throughout Matthew 6.

The Lord then emphasized that a fast is not intended for others to see. Professor and author Donald S. Whitney expounds on the Lord's instruction saying, "The only Observer of your fast should be the Secret One. No one else should know that you are fasting unless it is absolutely unavoidable or necessary. If you are married, or if someone regularly cooks for you, courtesy may require that you tell your spouse or someone else about your fast. The problem is not whether another person knows or asks about your fast, but whether you *want* him or her to know or ask so that you can appear more spiritual."[3] As with most spiritual matters, it's how we present our hearts before the Lord that is most important. We should fast not for recognition, but to draw near to and seek the will of the Lord.

One of my biggest revelations about fasting is that we're not required to pray during every moment of the fast. Yes, we are to pray without ceasing and stay in constant communion with God (1 Thess. 5:16–17). But that's whether we're currently fasting or not. When we fast, we are to go about our other, routine daily activities, just as normal but without food. When the hunger pangs strike, it's a reminder for us to seek the Lord, and then we are to pray as he leads. We can use the time we would have spent preparing or eating a meal as time devoted to prayer.

As 1 Thessalonians 5:23 teaches us, we are spirit, soul, and body. In that order. It reminds us that we are first spiritual beings and then physical beings. This is also emphasized in Job 10:11, which indicates that God clothed our spiritual beings with skin and flesh. The spirit was first and was clothed with the body.

It is important that we feed our spirits. It seems counterintuitive to feed something by withholding food, but that's exactly how we feed our spirits. By depriving ourselves of food, we are agreeing with God that our spiritual needs come before our physical needs. Believe me, there is great power and freedom in putting action to this idea.

Now, a fast does not have to take place over a long period of time. My favorite length of fast in this particular season of my life is from dinner on one day through breakfast the next day. I break the fast at lunch. All in all, I skip two meals and sleep through several hours of the fast. When you seek the Lord regarding how long to fast, I'm certain he'll provide you with an appropriate length of time.

It's very helpful for me to have a purpose behind my fast. Perhaps I'm seeking deliverance of some sort for a loved one. Or spiritual clarity for an upcoming decision I need to make. As a writer and teacher, I often fast and seek the Lord's face for clear direction on a message. I will write the purpose of my fast in my calendar, then journal the promptings I receive from the Holy Spirit. These frequently come straight out of the Bible, and because I'm listening to the Spirit with deliberate intent, I discern his direction as it pertains to what I seek.

This is what I mean by saying I feel as if a fast helps me "tune into the Holy Spirit." Tremendous clarity and discernment come when I'm physically hungry and spiritually fed. It's undeniable direction from the Lord, and I've learned to treasure it immensely.

Fasting is not just for our Jewish friends and didn't end after Queen Esther's time. It's expectation for all of us is delineated in Scripture (Mt 6:16-17). A fast is not presented in God's Word as an optional practice, yet it's often neglected in our society.

We rob ourselves of great blessing when we ignore the instruction to fast. Such blessings include the following:

- A deeper yearning for God. When we acknowledge that we need God more than we need food, it intensifies our desire for and our communion with the Lord.

- A heart filled with praise. By focusing on God rather than our meals, we can better see the wonder of what God provides in our very midst. Things that are simple and routine begin to seem supernatural—and they are! It becomes easy to praise the Lord in spirit and truth when we more readily see his wonders.

- Lasting satisfaction. When we're filled by God, it is satisfying on a far deeper level than providing food to our bodies. We're not hungry for him again in a few hours because he fills us to overflowing with his presence. And when we fast, that filling is ongoing, like an infinity pool.

- Clarity. I shared about this above: we can suddenly better hear and discern God's direction. We have better sensitivity to his leading.

- Physical benefits. There are many physical advantages to fasting, such as lowering LDL (bad) cholesterol, promoting muscle building, normalizing insulin sensitivity, slowing the aging process, and more.[4] It's no surprise that fasting is good for us because, after all, God invented it. Note: If you have health concerns, please seek medical advice before beginning a fast.

Yes, we should fast. We know this. Sometimes, however, it feels necessary to seek the Lord and ask for the desire to fast, along with a heart to honor him in and through it.

As we will see, Queen Esther found the three-day fast effective. And we will surely see blessings from fasting too, regardless of its duration. If your health and medical condition allow, give it a try. You may not do it well the first time or two that you attempt it, but as you progress and begin to experience its blessings and effectiveness, you won't regret it!

Digging Deeper

1. We are blessed to have a holy King who, unlike a Persian king, welcomes us to reveal our burdens and sorrow and share them with him. Write Matthew 11:28–30 in the space below (write from memory if you are able):

2. How does God's availability to those who are suffering differ from the attitudes of King Ahasuerus and other kings who were sheltered from suffering? Read 2 Samuel 1:11–12. How does Hannah's behavior compare with that of Mordecai in Esther 4:1? What does the comparison suggest?

3. What was accomplished by Mordecai's public mourning? Jews all over Persia mourned with fasting, weeping, and wailing, many with sackcloth and ashes. Why did Mordecai go to the king's gate?

4. In all of Mordecai's grief, do you believe he exaggerated the truth or overstated any of the information delivered to Esther through her servant Hathach?

5. What is the purpose of fasting, according to the following verses?

   • Ezra 8:21–23

   • Psalm 35:13–14

   • Daniel 9:3–20

6. Does fasting bring a guarantee of God's favor and blessing? (Perhaps the next question will help you answer.)

7. According to the following verses, what type of heart and attitude are to accompany fasting?

   • Isaiah 58:1–10

- Joel 2:12–13

- Matthew 6:16–18

8. Consider the timing of the fast in Esther.

   - It was during Passover. What implications, if any, did this pose for the Jews of Susa? How might a national disaster interrupt a holiday celebration today?

   - The king had not summoned Esther for thirty days and she may have believed she had lost his favor. What effect would a three-day fast have on Esther's appearance?

   - If she were already concerned about losing the favor of the king, how might this exacerbate the problem?

9. When Esther counted the cost, what did she find . . .

   - . . . if she approached the king?

- . . . if she did not approach the king?

- Why do you believe she was willing to pay the price?

10. Compare Esther 4:16 to Acts 20:24. What similarities do you find?

11. What is the cost of following God in your own life? What might you lose?

12. Is the cost worth the outcome? What is gained by following Christ?

13. Read Psalm 37 and describe how it could have been Mordecai's song.

- When you feel troubled or distressed, what do you try to remember that brings you peace or strength?

- It sometimes helps to set ourselves up for success and decide in advance how we'll act when a particular situation arises. In order to set yourself up for success in times of future struggle, prayerfully consider writing a letter to yourself in a notebook or Journal. Plan to read it during a trial or difficult circumstance. It might mimic Psalm 37 in some ways.

- How will you stand firm and remind yourself that God is in control?

14. As you read and meditated on Scripture, what insights did you that you can apply to your life? What promptings did you feel from the Holy Spirit as you studied?

Points to Ponder

In the Digging Deeper section of Chapter 1, I encouraged you to meditate on the Scriptures as if you were one of the characters in the book Esther. I asked, "how would you feel as events unfold? What sights and smells might you experience? What would you think? How would you react? Put yourself into the story and consider the details as if you were living them personally."

I'd venture to guess that you chose to consider history as through the eyes of Queen Esther. After all, she's the hero of the story and we can more easily relate to her as women, can't we?

Now, however, put yourself into Mordecai's sandals. Here's a man who made a bold move and took a stand for God. Because of his faith, he refused to bow before Haman. That boldness had severe consequences that affected not only Mordecai, but the entire Jewish nation.

Some scholars believe that Mordecai felt responsible for Haman's wrath against the Jews. They imply that he regretted his refusal to show homage to Haman. How might you feel if you were Mordecai?

Now look to God's Word. Do you see evidence of a remorseful Mordecai in Scripture? Read ahead to Esther 5:9 for additional insight. What did Mordecai discover as he counted the cost?

The words in Esther 4:14, "for such a time as this," are considered some of the most quoted in all of Scripture; they are certainly the most quoted words in the book of Esther. Why is this statement so inspirational? What does it signify in your own life? Why do you believe that God placed you on the earth at this particular time on the kingdom calendar? What do you believe he wants to accomplish through you? How will you respond to his call on your life?

CHAPTER 6

Come

Please re-read Esther chapters 4 and 5 before you continue.

Q ueen Esther faced a terrible dilemma. The protection of her people rested squarely and solely on her shoulders. She knew she could lose her life for her actions but made the decision to approach the king. Settle into this thinking: the queen feared she would be killed for interrupting her husband, that she would incur the death penalty for visiting him at work.

This wasn't an irrational fear. It was in accordance with the king's law. Scholars believe that the reason behind the law was protection of the king from those who wished to kill him. That may hold some logic, but it was extreme. There was just *one* consequence that applied to *every* man or woman who approached the king in the inner courtyard without a summons: death. Wife or not.

The queen feared she would be killed for interrupting her husband, that she would incur the death penalty for visiting him at work.

There was an exception in which Queen Esther had the smallest measure of hope. The king could choose to allow an interruption by extending his scepter as a show of approval. How often the king made such exceptions is unknown. Throughout the book of Esther we see evidence that he sometimes showed mercy, but his mercy ebbed and flowed like the tide. Ahasuerus was a fickle king, ruled by his own emotions and acting as his moods determined. Imagine the heavy dose of anxiety this brought to a wife preparing to talk with him.

> *Queen Esther had the smallest*
> *measure of hope.*

From Persia to Present Day

Now consider another sovereign ruler, our heavenly king. Those who approached God the Father in Old Testament times also feared for their lives. As God said to Moses in Exodus 33:20, "You cannot see My face, for no man can see Me and live!" (NASB). God made provision, and the only way for the priests to approach him was through the cleansing work of a blood sacrifice. Priests who entered the Holy Place and the Holy of Holies were required to exercise considerable measures of sacrifice and cleansing. Bells were sewn into their tunics to provide an audible signal if a priest were struck dead in the presence of God.

Let us examine God's character. Exodus 15:11 reveals God's majestic holiness: "Lord, who is like You among the gods? Who is like You, glorious in holiness, revered with praises, performing wonders?" The term "holy" means set apart, or separated.[1] God is completely separated and set apart from evil. As 1 John 1:5 says, "God is light and there is absolutely no darkness in Him." Because of his holiness, it is against God's very nature to dwell in the presence of, or overlook, sin. God hates sin and must judge it.

We live in a fallen world where people are sinful. All of us are sinful. Anything that you and I think, say, and do that is displeasing to the Lord is called sin. By our sin we are eternally separated from God, apart from the redemptive work of the cross, which served as the ultimate and final blood sacrifice. In his steadfast mercy and through a monumental act of love, God provided an intermediary who, by his blood, provides ongoing forgiveness of sin and reconciliation with God. Through Jesus Christ, he made a way.

To Queen Esther, King Ahasuerus extended his gold scepter. The king said, "Come."

To his children, God the Father extended the cross of Christ. Our King says, "Come."

Our King says, "Come."

Stepping into His courts

As I began studying Esther, verse 2 in chapter 5 brought immediate goose bumps. It still does. For weeks I had no idea why this verse stirred such emotion, and then the Holy Spirit revealed a striking correlation to my own life.

I imagine myself in this scene. I am, ever so timidly, approaching the King—not a king of earthly royalty but God the Father, the Lord of Hosts. I step into his courts as he, the sovereign ruler of heaven and earth, sits in the throne room. I am unworthy to approach him and, because of my sinful nature, have no business standing in his holy presence. I know my past; I know my present; and without question, so does he. I do not belong in the throne room.

Instead of striking me dead where I stand, God offers an intermediary. He chooses to provide a way of reconciliation and holds out the cross of Christ. I deserve death, but the Lord shows mercy and grace. He demonstrates his love for me in this: that while I was yet sinning, Christ died for me (see Rom. 5:8). Can you imagine yourself in this same scene?

Dressing for a King

Esther dressed carefully before visiting the king. We must also be attentive to our garment selection as we approach the Holy One. Let's look to Scripture to see what we should put on:

- "I greatly rejoice in the Lord, I exult in my God; for He has clothed me with garments of salvation and wrapped me in a robe of righteousness, as a groom wears a turban and as a bride adorns herself with her jewels" (Isa. 61:10).

- "For as many of you as have been baptized into Christ have put on Christ like a garment" (Gal. 3:27).

When King Ahasuerus extended mercy, Esther's response was extraordinary. She approached him and touched the tip of the scepter. Esther accepted the king's invitation and touched his offer of grace just as we must accept Christ and receive the gift of reconciliation that God offers. When we accept his offer of salvation, we carefully and deliberately clothe ourselves in Christ.

Cue the goose bumps. Can you feel them too?

Digging Deeper

1. Chapter 5 of Esther begins with incredible words: "Now it came about on the third day . . ." (NASB). To regain our point of reference, look back at Esther 4:16. What does the timing represent? The third day of what?

2. In biblical times, periods of distress and anguish as well as relief and revelation often came on the third day. Let's examine how this is supported in Scripture:

   - In Genesis 22:1–4, what was revealed to Abraham on the third day?

   - In Exodus 19:10–20, who appeared on the third day?

   - Look up Hosea 6:1–2. What appears to take place on the first and second days? What occurs on the third day?

   - In Matthew 20:19, what happens on the third day?

3. According to Esther 5:1–2, what took place on the third day? Do you see evidence of relief or revelation? Explain.

4. Unlike approaching the king of Persia, we need not wonder if our priestly King will allow us to approach. Please review as many of the following Scriptures (in context) as your time allows. The more you review, the richer your understanding will become. Record your insights in the space provided.

   - Exodus 24:12

   - Psalm 71:3

   - Psalm 102:1

- Matthew 14:28–29

- Matthew 16:24

- Matthew 19:14

- Matthew 19:21

- Luke 6:47

- Luke 14:26

- John 5:39–40

- John 6:35–37

- John 6:45

- John 7:37

- Revelation 3:20

5. I pray that your heart thrills to the King's call to come. Record your prayer of response to his call in a journal.

6. Is it more than crisis that motivates you to seek God? What else motivates you to pray? In what ways can you develop a more consistent prayer life?

7. Why is it important to balance prayer with action as we follow God?

8. Why didn't Esther immediately tell the king about Haman's plot and her own heritage?

9. What evidence of God's sovereignty do you see throughout this chapter of Esther?

10. As you read and meditated on Scripture, what insights did you gain that you can apply to your life? What promptings did you feel from the Holy Spirit as you studied?

Points to Ponder

Three times King Ahasuerus said to Queen Esther, "Whatever you want, even to half the kingdom, will be given to you." (Est. 5:3, 5:6, 7:2). Allow yourself to imagine what Esther could have demanded with such a generous offer from the king.

Queen Esther showed tremendous restraint and emotional self-control as she sat with the king and Haman at the banquet. Consider the fear, the hatred, the angst, and the turmoil she must have felt. How would you behave in such a situation, sitting with two men who planned to kill all the people in your family lineage? What words might you use? Like me, would you have trouble holding back tears?

How do you believe Esther's restraint worked in her favor?

Why do you think Queen Esther, in verse 8, postponed her request for one more day?

As hard as this might be, put yourself in Haman's shoes for a few minutes. Re-read verse 9. Have you ever had your joy and gladness stripped away in an instant when someone didn't behave as you had hoped?

Is there someone in your life that you wish would figuratively bow to you or give you the respect you feel you deserve? This may be a tough question, but consider it carefully, with an honest and transparent heart before the Lord. Seek his holy opinion on the matter, and ask that he reveal the reality of your heart to you. Before we judge the evil Haman too harshly, let's walk through some truthful self-examination in this regard. We may find some similarities in our own lives that require repentance and redemption.

CHAPTER 7

The Game Changer

Please re-read Esther chapters 5 and 6 before you continue.

*O*ur family loves sports. Some people don't understand the fascination, but it is difficult for me to imagine a life without it. I grew up loving (for many years even idolizing) the Denver Broncos. My parents' first date was at a Broncos game in the 1960s.

One of the things I love about watching sporting events is that the outcome of a game is unpredictable. It's a thrilling reality. Either team can win on any given day which is why games are played.

On some game days, we cheer for our favorite team even while sensing that losing is inevitable. Our loyalty demands that we root for them come rain, snow, shine, win, lose, or draw. One tremendously cold Sunday, the frigid temperatures tested my loyalty to its limit. Mike and I sat in the stands watching a Broncos game. When I reached for a sip of my diet soda and realized it was frozen solid, I turned to him and said, "It's time to go!"

We sat in our seats, shivering together, until we received tangible evidence that we may have crossed a reasonable boundary. Why is it so hard to pull ourselves away from a game?

A Game Changer

When the scoreboard isn't cooperating with our wishes, we wait with bated breath for something that shifts the momentum from one team to the other. It's called a "game changer." It can seem insignificant at the moment. Only when reviewing highlights do we recognize that a single, isolated event led to an entirely different outcome than expected.

Game changers frequently come in the midst of routine plays from competitors who remain consistent. They don't allow themselves to lose composure when circumstances look grim. A game changer is not necessarily a great play or outstanding effort of a great athlete. It can come from an outside source, such as a decision from a referee or equipment manager. Depending on the sport, a game changer can look like an ordinary first down, blocked shot, or strikeout that eventually reshapes the final score. It often marks the beginning of the turning point.

> *Only when reviewing highlights do we recognize that a single, isolated event led to an entirely different outcome than expected.*

Sometimes because of a single play, a second accomplishment follows, then another, and our once-losing team pulls out an astonishing victory. I'll admit, the possibility keeps me glued to the bleachers, even when they're as cold as ice cubes.

If the plight of the Jews in ancient Persia were the game, the book of Esther would be the highlight film. We might examine each event in replay and wonder where the momentum changed to favor the Jews. They faced the annihilation of their entire race; they were in essence losing the biggest game of their lives. By the end of the story, they triumphed over an evil enemy with a malicious ploy. The victory of the Jews hinged on what's described in Esther 6:1. Therein lies our game changer: the king had insomnia.

Talk about a routine occurrence that had profound impact. It barely seems worth discussing until we see what the king did overnight. He had the records of his reign read back to him from the book that documented the daily events of his kingdom.

> *If the plight of the Jews were the game, the book of Esther would be the highlight film.*

It Just So Happened

There are many ways a sleepless king could amuse himself in the middle of the night: entertaining concubines, listening to royal musicians, or enjoying a warm, comforting glass of milk. But God ordained that King Ahasuerus review the chronicles to show him he had overlooked something significant. The King of the universe revealed something vital to King Ahasuerus during that wakeful night. The rest is history.

It "just so happened" that while the king listened to the story of his reign, Haman was in the palace courtyard. The prime minister was working the night shift to ensure proper construction of the gallows that would display the execution of Mordecai. Haman was so driven by the thought of the execution, he personally supervised the midnight mission.

Scholars believe that when the king asked Haman how to honor a man in Esther 6:6, it was still pitch dark outside. Haman was likely waiting for daylight so that he could present the king with his request for execution. Instead he received a summons into the king's bed chamber to answer a game-changing question. In one of the most significant ironies in the entire book, Haman is ordered to honor his enemy, Mordecai, and parade him through the city square.

The text leaves us wondering what Mordecai must have thought about all of this. The king ordered the destruction of all Jews; then a few days later he had Mordecai publicly honored for his act of valiant service to the throne—five years after the fact. And Verse 10 of chapter 6 indicates the king even knew of Mordecai's Jewish heritage. I have to believe Mordecai recognized God's sovereign hand at play.

I love the observation made by pastor and Bible teacher Warren Wiersbe: at the conclusion of the parade, Mordecai "returned to his place at the gate and continued to serve the king. Applause doesn't change truly humble people, for their values are far deeper."[1] Mordecai stayed true to himself while Haman, with his crushed pride, went home grieving and covering his head and was later whisked away, unknowingly to his final meal.

> *"Applause doesn't change truly humble people, for their values are far deeper."* —Warren Wiersbe

From Persia to Present Day

Have you ever wished for a game changer in your own life? During times when things look bad, it appears that victory is out of reach, and it feels like you can't go on—have you longed for a breakthrough?

I have too. And I found something that effects change more often than not. It's worship. I know. You thought I'd say prayer, didn't you?

Yes. Prayer changes things. Most often, change through prayer takes time to come about. But sometimes we need a change agent that works in a more immediate manner. So of course, pray! Watch with expectation for the Lord's work, knowing sometimes he does move immediately. And worship too. It may not change our circumstance, but it can immediately change the way we view it. And that can change everything.

Bible Teacher and Author, Sheila Walsh commented in her recent Bible study *The Longing in Me* "How do we live through tough times? What do you do when the road ahead is a long one? How do we look to God alone as our source of strength? We worship. Even when there is no light on the path, or dawn on the horizon, we worship God."[2]

God inhabits the praise of his people (see Ps. 22:3 KJV). When we worship, we're drawn into the Lord's presence and as a sweet friend and sister described, "Worship trains the flesh to be quiet and the Spirit to prevail." I love that. She shared her personal experience this way: "Worship reveals the place of awesome wonder and power where God fights for me."

Wow. That makes me want to take a break from our study and worship. Go ahead if you're feeling that way too, but come right back!

When we worship through trials and difficult situations, we declare in the heavenly realm that God's plan is perfect and his ways are good. It's an act of surrender—of bowing low to exalt the name of the Most High God even while we struggle. Worship is the act of moving our focus from longing to change our circumstance to longing for God alone. It's a powerful practice. It's putting our physical needs and fleshly worries aside so that he is honored even while we step in faith to face what terrifies us most.

My husband Mike spent nearly his entire working life employed by our local sheriff's office. When it came time for the current sheriff to retire, we strongly felt the Lord's prompting that Mike should pursue the position of sheriff. He had climbed the ranks of the agency during his twenty-seven years of service and at that point was third in command.

A sheriff is an elected official, which meant Mike would be jumping into the political arena. Neither of us had the slightest desire to become politically active, yet the prompting from the

Lord would not ease. We knew we must continue down the path God had illuminated.

Early on, there were five contestants in the race for sheriff. In the steps leading up to the primary, Mike was required to participate at our county assembly where our political party would determine which candidates they would support. We had never done anything like this before, and I'm not ashamed to say that we were shaking in our boots. Politics have a way of bringing meanness out of people, and Mike's thin-skinned wife had a lot of trouble facing critics.

In the weeks leading up to the county assembly, my mentor shared a Scripture passage with me. She had no idea how it would touch my heart, but as I read it, I felt the Holy Spirit's prompting: "This is for you. Get ready."

The passage was 2 Chronicles 20. The gist is this: King Jehoshaphat faced a mighty battle and he was afraid. In his fear, Jehoshaphat sought the Lord, who said,

> "Do not be afraid or discouraged because of this vast number, for the battle is not yours, but God's. Tomorrow, go down against them. You will see them coming up the Ascent of Ziz, and you will find them at the end of the valley facing the Wilderness of Jeruel. You do not have to fight this battle. Position yourselves, stand still, and see the salvation of the Lord. He is with you, Judah and Jerusalem. Do not be afraid or discouraged. Tomorrow, go out to face them, for Yahweh is with you."

> Then Jehoshaphat bowed with his face to the ground, and all Judah and the inhabitants of Jerusalem fell down before the Lord to worship Him. (2 Chron. 20:15–18)

"The battle is not yours, but God's"—2 Chron. 20:15

At the time I didn't know why, but the Lord hid this word in my heart and prompted me to meditate on it frequently.

When our small but loyal team of political supporters walked in to the county assembly, we were literally surrounded by the opposition. They were vast in their number, cheering and chanting, wearing T-shirts and carrying signs. It looked like a high school pep rally!

The Lord's Word came to life in an instant. Literally, we were facing a similar battle as Jehoshaphat. There was not a place on the premises where we didn't see obvious opposition, yet the Lord commanded, "Do not be afraid or discouraged. This battle is not yours, but God's."

As our team members looked at me with deer-in-the-headlight stares and facial expressions that conveyed, "There's no way we come out of here victorious," I encouraged them to worship. The room was far too loud to share the entire story with them, but I let them know the Lord had prepared us all for this and that above all we were to worship him that day! For he was with us! We were to be thankful for his provision and give him glory and honor throughout the day. I promised to share the whole story later but asked them, for now, to trust and worship. And so they did.

We made it out with victory. It was narrow—unbelievably narrow—but it was all that was needed to earn Mike a position on the primary ballot.

Our game changer was our willingness to worship God when things looked impossible. We joined together with our army and trusted him. We exalted his name, bowed down in surrender to his will, and humbled ourselves before him.

Worship, my friend. Even when you may not want to. And watch God unfold a victory tailor-made just for you.

Digging Deeper

1. According to Esther 5:11–12, in what did Haman place his confidence? What does Proverbs 28:26 say about such thinking?

2. When, like Haman, have you taken personal credit for that which the Lord provided? Consider a time when perhaps you looked at something in your life (such as a job, a child, a skill or talent, wealth, honor, promotion, recognition, faith, spiritual growth, etc.) and thought to yourself with pride, "I did that!"

3. Write John 3:27 in the space below.

4. Write James 1:17 in the space below.

5. How does Jeremiah 9:23–24 help us apply John 3:27 and James 1:17?

6. Revisit Proverbs 6:16–19. Does pride /arrogance appear on the list of things God hates?

7. Read the following verses and describe the events and circumstances that fueled the escalation of Haman's pride:

- Esther 3:1

- Esther 3:5

- Esther 3:6

- Esther 3:10–11

- Esther 3:15

- Esther 5:4

- Esther 5:9

- Esther 5:11–13

- Esther 6:6

8. Read Esther 6:6–9 (HCSB) here:

Haman entered and the king asked him, "What should be done for the man the king wants to honor?" Haman thought to himself, "Who is it the king would want to honor more than me?" Haman told the king, "For the man the king wants to honor: Have them bring a royal garment that the king himself has worn and a horse the king himself has ridden, which has a royal diadem on its head. Put the garment and the horse under the charge of one of the king's most noble officials. Have them clothe the man the king wants to honor, parade him on the horse through the city square, and proclaim before him, 'This is what is done for the man the king wants to honor."

- I've provided extra space in the text above so that you can add markings. Circle every occurrence of the words "king" and "royal."

- Underline or place a star next to the phrases "king wants to honor" and "king would want to honor."

- Wiersbe states, "If what is described in Esther 6:8–9 had actually been done for Haman, it would have given the people of Sushan the impression that Ahasuerus had chosen Haman to be his successor."[3] (See 1 Kings 1:28–40 for a similar instance in the Bible.)

  What evidence do you see in Esther 6 that Haman had at least daydreamed about being king?

9. Compare Esther 5:14 with Esther 6:12–13. Why do you believe Zeresh encouraged Haman to have Mordecai killed but later

declared that a Jew could not be overcome and Haman's own downfall was certain?

10. List the evidence you see in Esther chapters 5 and 6 of God's providence.

11. As you read and meditate on Scripture, what insights did you gain that you can apply to your life? What promptings did you feel from the Holy Spirit as you studied?

Points to Ponder

The tables certainly turned against Haman. There were several things that Haman planned to inflict upon Mordecai and the Jews that he experienced himself instead. It seems that the Lord gave Haman several warnings and every opportunity to repent. But because he pursued his own evil agenda, he encountered his day of destruction.

How can we as Christians discern a warning from the Lord in order to avoid a fate like Haman's?

Throughout the book of Esther, the Lord shows he is longsuffering. How do we see that the Lord's patience must not be confused with approval or tolerance?

CHAPTER 8

Removing Masks

Please re-read Esther 7 before you continue.

We live in a world of masks. We keep our true feelings covered, putting on masks and projecting happy faces and positive attitudes. We often silence our honest thoughts and vulnerabilities knowing that our culture sees them as weakness. Honesty represents fragility; authenticity is dangerous.

Perhaps you've heard some of these common sayings:

"Never let them see you sweat."

"Head up. Stay strong. Fake a smile. Move along."

"Smile, be happy. Never let them see how it hurt."

"I smile to hide that I'm completely overwhelmed."

Without a doubt, there are times we all adopt these attitudes. Sometimes we feel we need masks for more than a show of strength, and we are convinced we must wear them to protect those we love. We suppose that our own show of courage will somehow strengthen those around us.

I have a longtime friend who gave permission to share her story. Her husband was diagnosed with skin cancer one summer. The tumor was removed before I ever caught wind of the problem, as she mentioned it only after the fact. The following winter, however, he developed an unusual lump in his neck and sure enough, the melanoma had spread to his lymph nodes. As we talked, my friend maintained her strong demeanor, her "everything's fine" attitude, and projected a casual level of fearlessness before her children. She felt that her show of strength encouraged her husband, and I have no doubt that it did.

The new tumor required removal, and on the day of the surgery, I sent a text message to let her know I was praying. I urged her to walk in the Lord's strength instead of her own. I received the following reply:

"I keep trying cuz heaven knows I'm exhausted from keeping the brave face on when all I really want to do is curl up and cry."

The truth is, we can only keep up our appearances for so long. Exhaustion overtakes us. Eventually, our cracks reach the surface and our walls begin to crumble. Unless we loosen the valve and release some pressure, a volcano of emotion is bound to erupt.

Unless we loosen the valve and release some pressure, a volcano of emotion is bound to erupt.

The Lord Knows

I consider it a tremendous gift to serve a Lord who knows our every heartache. We can be real before Him—and display all of the gut-wrenching emotion that the world rejects. Not only can we display our true feelings to him, but also we're assured that his love will never fail. In our ugliest moments, the Lord remains our steadfast advocate, defender, friend, and shepherd.

I've tried to imagine Esther's emotions from the moment she learned of Haman's plot to destroy her people. Not only had she kept the profound secret of her heritage, but she now had to muster monumental courage on behalf of those who shared that heritage. She had to remove her mask to protect those she loved.

She portrayed a rare level of decorum and dignity, all while under pressures most of us will never experience in our lifetimes. When Esther counted the cost, she ended the charade and revealed all, becoming completely transparent and vulnerable with the king.

From Persia to Present Day

It occurs to me that Esther showed remarkable humility and grace. Throughout our time of study, we have yet to see her grumble or complain, even in the height of her dilemma.

From day to day, what we often try to portray as transparency can lead to grumbling if we allow it. We start off thinking we're letting off a little steam and sharing our true feelings on a short Facebook post. It feels safe, and yet before we know it, we've thrown someone we care about under the proverbial bus. We're aware that the truth can sting, so we sometimes try to soften the blow through sarcasm or coarse jesting. It's not a healthy habit.

This is not the type of transparency we pursue before the Lord and others. And this is not what Esther modeled.

The Lord convicted me, years ago, about the way I degraded my husband through what I believed were humorous (albeit sarcastic) remarks among friends. I am exceedingly grateful for the way God gently and gradually revealed how much I was hurting the man I love. Not only did the Holy Spirit bring conviction; he helped me stop and begin to honor my husband instead. I began by choosing my words more carefully when I spoke of him.

It might have been easy for Esther to deride the king, pointing out that he had overlooked a rather important detail with his latest decree. If I were in Esther's shoes, I would likely have made underhanded comments in hopes that he would catch my drift. Instead, Esther patiently waited for the perfect moment and presented truth without exaggeration or mockery. When she spoke, her words were concise, well chosen, and effectively communicated. They achieved the desired effect.

This is a trait of Esther that I deeply admire. We can portray dignity and grace at all times, remembering there is more love inside of us than we realize. Even when we don't feel like it or when it seems difficult, we can treat others with respect and honor. How? By walking in the strength of Jesus and allowing his love to flow through us. Remembering to see others as Jesus does helps us to treat them with love and respect.

> *There is more love inside of us than we realize.*

Not only is this a way to portray gentleness and kindness, both of which are fruit of the Holy Spirit dwelling in us, but it's also an effective communication tool. Showing honor and respect helps diffuse a situation rather than escalate it and paves the way for our thoughts to be heard and received by their intended recipient. It can help us avoid conflict and walk in unity.

The Masks We Wear

Consider this question honestly: what masks are you wearing right this moment?

Are you covering up your struggle with anger? Or hiding behind shame? Were you a victim and continue to feel dirty and disgraced? Have you known the scorn of rejection? Is there a sin in your life that has a hold on you, yet you're too embarrassed (or prideful) to share the truth with a trusted sister?

We want to fit in. We want to feel accepted and loved. Deep down we believe that those around us would never offer their friendship if they knew the ugly truth. If they only knew our hidden secrets, they would never welcome us into their lives . . . or their homes . . . or their churches. So we keep our past—and sometimes our present—hidden from view. We put on our masks and portray ourselves to be just like everyone else.

The problem is that we're portraying a lie. All of us have things in our lives that we're not proud of. We've made mistakes. We've sinned. We've not only disappointed others; we've hurt them. There's a story behind our masks that those around us can identify with—if we would only allow it.

If we would give others a chance, open up our lives, and share honestly within safe and trusted environments, we would find freedom to a degree that we have never experienced. We would learn what it means to feel unconditional love. It's what Christ offers us every day, and he often reveals it through those he brings into our lives.

What if, like Esther and Mordecai, we took off our masks and showed the world who we really are? What if we walked in confidence knowing that we are fearfully and wonderfully made by the Lord himself? What if we allowed the beauty of his glory to shine through us? What if, when we shared the pain and ugliness of our past, another sister was encouraged? What if you could help her find freedom and healing through your testimony? Would you do it? What's holding you back?

Please know that I'm not recommending that you confess every sin of your past over the public address system at a filled-to-capacity stadium. Not everyone needs to hear it all. But I believe the Lord brings trusted companions into each of our lives. (If you can't think of one by name, ask the Lord to show her to you. He will!) Maybe she's a mentor or the one who sits next to you in Bible study every week. Pray and ask the Lord to guide you to a trusted friend with whom you can share your real truth.

Let's not allow Satan to keep us in the bondage of shame any longer. Let's let in Jesus—the Light of the World—and allow him to knit our lives together with others and perform a healing work in our hearts.

Digging Deeper

1. Re-read Esther chapter 7. In verse 4, how had Esther and her people been "sold out" to death, destruction, and extermination? Refer to Esther 3:9–11 as you consider your answer.

2. As you imagine the king's fury, the tone of his voice, and his body language in verse 5, how do you believe he felt about the threat on Esther's life? In the king's own words, how did he describe the decree?

3. Consider the following as it relates to Esther's naming her enemy:

   • Why do you think she withheld Haman's name as she described her request to the king in verses 3-4?

   • Why did she name Haman in verse 6? (Verse 5 provides a clue)

   • How did Esther describe Haman in verse 6?

   4. Fill in the blanks below from verse 6 (HCSB) and answer the following related questions:

- Haman stood terrified before the _____ and _____.

- What do you see as the significance of the term "king and queen"?

- Have we seen the couple referred to in this capacity before?

- Does it imply a sense of unity between husband and wife?

- What might a unified king and queen meant from Haman's point of view?

5. How do we see a sudden protective stance from the king toward Esther?

   - In verse 5:

   - In verse 7:

   - In verse 8:

6. Why might the king have needed a walk to process the news he had just received (see verses 5 through 7)?

7. Read Galatians 6:7–8. What does it mean to reap what we sow?

    - Jacob killed an animal and lied to his father. Compare Genesis 27:1–9 and 37:31–35. How did Jacob reap what he sowed?

    - Pharaoh ordered the drowning of Jewish male babies. How did Pharaoh reap what he sowed when comparing Exodus 1 to Exodus 15:4?

    - Even Saul of Tarsus (who became Paul) reaped what he sowed. Compare Acts 7:54–8:1 and 14:19 and explain how.

8. Haman wanted Mordecai to bow before him (see Est. 3:5-6). In what physical position was Haman when his face was covered? (See Est. 7:7–9).

9. In the verses you just read (Est. Est. 3:5–6 and Est. 7:7–9):

    - Who did Haman wish to destroy for an offense they did not commit?

- Did Haman commit the offense that the king accused him of?

- Why was the seventy-five-foot gallows constructed? (See Est. 5:14).

- Who was ultimately hanged on that gallows? (See Est. 7:9–10).

- Did Haman reap what he sowed?

10. In Genesis 26:12, how does the Lord provide blessing through sowing and reaping?

11. Read Galatians 6:8 as well as Matthew 10:42 and 25:31–46. How can we reap blessing?

12. As you read and meditated on Scripture, what insights did you gain that you can apply to your life? What promptings did you feel from the Holy Spirit as you studied?

Points to Ponder

In ancient Persia, there was a clear purpose for eunuchs: to protect a king's harem from contamination. No one but appointed eunuchs and the king himself could come close to a concubine, let alone the queen. Technically Haman should not have stayed in the presence of the queen after the king left the room. In quite a quandary, he literally threw himself at her and begged for his life. She did not extend mercy.

Some commentators hint that perhaps Esther should have shown mercy. What's your opinion on that? Was Haman showing remorse? Is remorse required in order to receive mercy?

Consider the eunuch Harbona. We met him first in Esther chapter 1. What do you imagine was the depth of his involvement with the king's activities? I have often considered the wealth of information that servants accumulate and how they must resist the temptation to speak up from time to time. Obviously Harbona reached a point where he could no longer hold his tongue. Does he seem to be an ally of Esther? Look back to Esther 2:15. How might the eunuch Hegai's alliance with Esther support your thoughts?

Lastly, how can you live mask-free day by day and encourage others to do the same? In other words, how can you live with transparency and honesty, allowing God to use your trials and tests as part of your testimony to others?

CHAPTER 9

A King Who Provides a Way

Please re-read Esther chapter 8 before you continue.

P salm 37:35-36 reads, "I have seen a wicked, violent man well-rooted like a flourishing native tree. Then I passed by and noticed he was gone; I searched for him, but he could not be found."

The evil adversary, Haman, was dead—killed by the king's men for planning to attack the Jews, including the king's wife. Yet his edict lived on. A royal edict could not be revoked once it was issued, as the law dictated. Even the king could not repeal the order to annihilate the Jews. It was issued by Haman, but because it was sealed by the royal ring, it was the same as if the king had written every word. It was permanent and everlasting.

King Ahasuerus, however, made another provision. He allowed Mordecai, his newly appointed prime minister, to write whatever pleased him in order to provide protection to the Jews—and to do so just as Haman had done: in the king's name.

There is another law as old as time that cannot be revoked: the law of sin and death. Our carnal, sinful nature leads to spiritual death (see Rom. 6:23). God will not rescind this law, which has been in force since the fall of Adam. Instead, through Christ, God provided a way of salvation. He gave a Savior to bear our sins and lay his life on the cross. Through the resurrection of Jesus Christ, God's children are set free from the law of sin and death because of the Spirit's law of life. Revel with me in the correlation:

> The Spirit's law of life in Christ Jesus has set you free from the law of sin and of death. What the law could not do since it was limited by the flesh, God did. He condemned sin in the flesh by sending His own Son in flesh like ours under sin's domain, and as a sin offering, in order that the law's requirement would be accomplished in us who do not walk according to the flesh but according to the Spirit. (Rom. 8:2–4)

God Makes a Way

"What the law could not do . . .
God did."—Romans 8:3

God made a way for the Jews of Persia where there seemed to be no way. He delivered life when it seemed the Jews were destined to annihilation.

Similarly, he made a way for us to walk in victory over sin when it seemed we were destined to a life of bondage under the law. I love the HCSB wording of Romans 8:3: "What the law could not do . . . God did."

For the Jews in Persia, what King Ahasuerus could not do, God did through Mordecai. This is true for our society today as well. What our government and laws cannot accomplish, God can. Living by the laws of man is vital to our society, but it doesn't make a way for us to spend eternity with God in heaven. Jesus alone is our hope for eternity. We place our confidence in him and continue to trust in his sovereignty. In that hope, we have reason to rejoice and celebrate.

Esther 8:16 says that "the Jews celebrated with gladness, joy, and honor." With the delivery of Mordecai's new edict, the Jews became ready to avenge themselves against their enemies. Not only could they protect their families and property; it was now common knowledge that the queen was of their Semitic heritage, and the king's new prime minister was a devout Jew as well.

Clearly this was not the end of the nation of Israel. God was not finished with his people and had demonstrated his might through powerful, albeit ordinary, methods. These were great reasons to celebrate by anyone's estimation!

> *God demonstrated his might through powerful, albeit ordinary, methods.*

From Persia to Present Day

I can still hear the voice of a beloved man, all these years later. His words held no measure of animosity nor hint of arrogance. He stated them as a matter of fact: "I ain't a sinner."

I have no idea how many times my dad uttered those words. He sincerely believed that because he had never murdered or stolen from anyone, nor spent time in jail, he was without sin. From time to time he explained that he followed the Ten Commandments. I believe that he believed he did. But truth be told, I'm not sure he knew all ten of those commandments by heart. He was one who commonly used language that profaned the Lord's name specifically. Therein lies at least one point etched on the stone tablets toward which Dad's aim missed the mark. I've missed that particular mark too.

Before I continue, you need to know that there is no gal on earth who loved her daddy more than this one. He was my hero in more ways than I can count. He simply didn't know Jesus and had no desire to know him. The term "Born Again Christian" was uttered only with disdain when the topic came up. It truly boiled down to the fact that Dad didn't see himself as a sinner and didn't want anyone trying to convince him that he was. If a person is not a sinner, why in the world would they need a Savior?

Now maybe you have no trouble acknowledging the fact that sin is in all of us by our human nature.

Or maybe, like some, you struggle to see yourself as one who acts in ways that aren't pleasing to God. Your work hard, you pray, you give financially to the church, and you follow the laws of man. You consider yourself a good person and would never go so far as to refer to yourself as a sinner.

The *Lexham Bible Dictionary* defines sin as "human activity that is contrary to God's will."[1] That action can consist of things that we do, or things we say, or—here's the kicker—even things we think. Ouch.

It's interesting to watch the progressive description of sin in Scripture. 1 Corinthians 6:9–10 lists outward behaviors. Galatians 5:19–21 repeats some of those behaviors and adds attitudes and ambitions to the list. Ephesians 2:1–3 then includes inclinations and thoughts.

So if we think that we would like to do such-and-such to so-and-so, we've just sinned, even if we never intend to act on such thinking. And that time last week when you blurted out a bad word as that other driver cut you off, that was sin too. I know, you hadn't planned to say that word, but out it came. It's evidence of the sin that lives deep inside of all of us.

Is there anyone in your life that you've pleased and honored perfectly, 100 percent of the time? I didn't think so. We are human and we disappoint one another. We make mistakes, whether we intend to or not. And just as we can't please each other all the time, we can't always please God either. On each occasion that we fall short, well, the Bible calls that sin.

We make mistakes, whether we intend to or not.

The Bible teaches that "just as sin entered the world through one man [Adam], and death through sin, in this way death spread to all men, because all sinned" (Rom. 5:12).

It teaches that all of us have turned away. There is not one who does good—not one (Rom. 3:12). Moreover, as Paul explains, "All have sinned and fall short of the glory of God" (Rom. 3:23).

It's clear throughout Scripture that I'm a sinner. You're a sinner. And my beloved dad? He was a sinner too.

There is good news. God loves us in our sinful states and provides grace. What a beautiful truth. He's our heavenly Father, after all. You still love your kids when they blow it, don't you? God does too. And while we were yet sinners, Jesus voluntarily laid down his life for us (Rom. 5:8).

We know that because of God's great love he provided his son to shed his blood on the cross. Jesus was the ultimate sacrifice, providing a way for sinful people (remember, that's all of us) to reconcile with a holy God. After the list of transgressions named in 1 Corinthians 6:9-10, verse 12 reminds us that we are washed, sanctified, and justified (in other words, we are made clean—as clean as if we had never sinned in the first place) "in the name of the Lord Jesus Christ and by the Spirit of our God."

God made a way. And I'm overjoyed to let you know that my dad saw and accepted God's gift before it was too late. To God alone be the glory. In Christ and through the forgiveness of sins, we have reason to rejoice and be glad!

God made a way.

Digging Deeper

Haman was dead. Esther was awarded his estate. Mordecai entered the king's presence because Esther revealed their relationship.

1. Please read Esther 8:1 in the NASB, provided here (italics mine): "On that day, King Ahasuerus gave the house of Haman, the enemy of the Jews, to Queen Esther; and Mordecai came before the king, for Esther had disclosed *what he was to her*." After our weeks together studying Esther, how would you describe what Mordecai was to Esther? Look beyond their blood relation and try to communicate, through Esther's point of view, what Mordecai meant to her.

2. What would she have wanted the king to understand about their relationship? Record your thoughts below.

3. When the king was made to understand what Mordecai was to Esther, how did he respond? (See Est. 8:2). What additional concession did Esther make (also in Est. 8:2)?

4. At this point, Esther had not yet received all she had hoped for from the king. What additional petition did Esther make? (Est. 8:3-6).

5. What emotion did Esther show?

   - How did her display of emotion differ from the previous times when Esther addressed the king?

- Scripture does not indicate that Esther had children, nor does it indicate that Esther was barren. As a married woman, it's very possible that by this time, Esther was a mother. How would Esther's love as a mother stir her emotions as she pleaded with the king for the lives of her people?

6. How do you interpret the king's attitude in Esther 8:7? Look at several Bible translations of this verse if you are able, and answer accordingly. Was he annoyed by Esther's pleading? Sympathetic? Apathetic? On what do you base your interpretation?

7. What haste do you see in Esther 8:7–10 and 8:14? Why do you believe Mordecai hurried to deliver the new edict? What do you think we could learn today from Mordecai and his couriers?

8. Compare and contrast Mordecai's edict with that of Haman in Esther 3:13–15.

   - What were the similarities and differences in the wording and commands of the two edicts?

   - What were the similarities and differences in the ways the edicts were delivered?

- What were the similarities and differences in the urgency levels of delivering the messages?

- What were the similarities and differences in the responses of the people? (See also question 10).

9. Read Esther 8:11 in several different Bible translations. Was Mordecai's intent that Persian women and children were to be killed? If Mordecai made allowance for the destruction of any women and children who were hostile to the Jews, what benefit would that provide?

10. What is the difference between the Jews avenging themselves and seeking revenge?

11. In Esther 8:15, it is recorded that Mordecai went from the king's presence wearing royal purple and white with a great gold crown and a purple robe of fine linen.

- How does this compare to the priest's attire in Exodus 28:1–6?

- What were the reasons for the garments specified in Exodus 28:2?

- The color purple represents royalty, kingship, and elegance. Examine the following Scriptures and record other uses of purple garments. Note your observations in the space provided.

    Judges 8:26

    Mark 15:17–18

    Luke 16:19

- Read the following passages and determine the use of fine linen:

    Genesis 41:41–42

    Chronicles 15:25–27

    Proverbs 31:24

    Luke 23:52–53

    Luke 24:12

- From the following cross references, record your insights about the overlap of royalty and priesthood. Also, make a note of the group of people to which each passage refers.

  Exodus 19:6

  1 Peter 2:5–10

  Revelation 1:6

12. Compare Esther 4:1–2 with Esther 8:15–16. How complete was the restoration of the emotion of the Jewish people? After the communication of Mordecai's edict, did you sense that mourning continued?

13. Let's look at other biblical examples of restoration provided by the Lord. Read each Scripture (in context) and record what you learn about restoration, healing, and God's generous provision at the conclusion of a difficult trial.

  - Job 42:10 (compare Job 41:12 with Job 1:2–3)

  - Psalm 71:20–21

- Isaiah 61:7

- Joel 2:25–26

- Luke 4:18–19

- Acts 3:19–26

- 1 Peter 5:10

- Revelation 21:1–8

- How does God's restoration throughout history encourage you in your daily walk? As you face a trial, does it help you to press on, knowing that the Lord sees every aspect of what you encounter and will make your situation whole by his standards and in his timing?

14. As you read and meditated on Scripture, what insights did you gain that you can apply to your life? What promptings did you feel from the Holy Spirit as you studied?

Points to Ponder

When God provides a way, he doesn't skimp on results. In Esther's time, God's restoration of the Jews was so complete, many Persians became Jewish proselytes. They weren't ashamed to be identified with the Jews, even though there were still enemies present. Wiersbe states that the Jews were "proud of their race and so happy with what God had done that they were attracting others to their faith. Even the pagan Gentiles could see that God was caring for his people in a remarkable way."[2]

What do you believe would be the result if today's Christians displayed more joy in the Lord? Do you believe that unbelievers can find Jesus attractive according to the way you display the joy of the Lord in your own life? What are some ways you can feel and express the joy of the Lord?

CHAPTER 10

Victorious!

Please re-read Esther chapters 9 and 10 before continuing.

*H*ow do you qualify a victory? By a score? Or an accomplishment? Do you consider yourself victorious when overcoming a challenging feat? Or navigating a trial while continuing to honor the Lord? Is a victory always obvious? Or might it sometimes look like defeat to a watching world?

Haman imposed a decree of genocide that, even after his demise, seemed impossible for the Jews to overcome. There were approximately one hundred million people in the Persian Empire, with about fifteen million Jews among them.[1] After Mordecai's decree, the Jews could defend themselves, but there were nearly six Persians to every Jew. It would seem that, even with the new decree that gave the Jews the right to assemble and defend themselves, they were still walking into a losing battle. There was no way they could win.

If the Jews desired to overtake the Persians and annihilate them as they themselves were slated to be destroyed, they missed the mark of victory. But for the Jews, victory didn't look at all like decimation of their enemy. Victory meant knowing that God remembered them when they had all but forgotten him.

It was remembering that they were his people and he was their God.

Victory was the reminder that the Lord was on their side and provided for their protection through his powerful yet unseen hand. Victory blossomed when the Jewish nation stood tall after the day of an irrevocable sentence of death. It made its mark when the people of Persia professed to be Jews, and when officials of the provinces assembled to fight alongside them rather than against them.

Victory meant knowing that God remembered them when they had all but forgotten him.

While the Jews were thrilled to feel free of their enemies, they didn't celebrate the number of casualties. They didn't plunder possessions or try to rise up as the new leaders of the Persian Empire. It was the day of rest—the day after the battle—that became the day of feasting and rejoicing. Purim was an impromptu festival, birthed by the victorious feeling of standing tall after expecting certain death. The threat was over and God's people celebrated the triumph over evil.

To this day, the Jews hold fast to the memorial celebration of Purim. Each year, the book of Esther is read in the Synagogue. It serves as a reminder that in every generation, there are those who will desire to rise up to destroy the Jews, but God prevails.

In every generation, there are those who will desire to rise up to destroy the Jews, but God prevails.

From Persia to Present Day

Victory. It can feel elusive, can't it? Some of us are struggling at home when battles escalate among loved ones. Some are fighting terminal illness wondering how we can ever walk in victory again. Financial woes plague our hearts and minds, distracting us from the day to day. We don't feel we can navigate another day in our struggle with infertility, or shame, or the worry we carry for our grown kids or aging parents.

The truth is, we're all facing something difficult. Every one of us faces a fight that we wish we could avoid somehow. We might feel as if we're alone, as if God is absent or has abandoned us in this journey we call life. Even if we're reluctant to admit it aloud, we sometimes feel as if we have no hope.

But in Christ, there is always hope. Esther's life offers proof. Even when we don't feel as if God is on our side, he is. He is faithful. Even when we don't see him moving in obvious ways, he continues to work behind the scenes. He is mighty.

God sees every detail that unfolds in our lives. Nothing is beyond his notice. Not one thing. The hangnail you bumped last evening? He saw that. And he knows the exact number of hairs that came out in your brush this morning too.

He looks upon it all with unconditional love and overwhelming compassion. Look with me at a few scriptural mentions of the Lord's great love and compassion:

- God describes himself as a compassionate and gracious God, slow to anger and rich in faithful love and truth (Ex. 34:6).

- We read in Psalm 103:13 that "as a father has compassion on his children, so the Lord has compassion on those who fear Him."

- He fed the five thousand because he felt compassion for them (Matt. 14:14).

- He restored the sight of the blind men because he was moved with compassion (Matt. 20:29–34).

- Jesus was deeply moved by the death of Lazarus and the grief of his sisters (John 11:33) and he wept (John 11:35).

- In 2 Corinthians 1:3 we see God as "the Father of mercies and the God of all comfort."

When our hearts hurt, his does too. He is for us. Our God will fight for us—even while we sleep. What he will accomplish is far and above what we could do on our own, so why not invite him into the midst of our trials?

He is for us. Our God will fight for us.

The Old Testament book of Esther presents a magnificent illustration of Romans 8:28: "We know that all things work together for the good of those who love God: those who are called according to His purpose."

Think of Esther's story as a tangled ball of string. The events are messy, nonsensical, and leave us wondering what good could ever come of them. As things unfold, that tangled ball of string is gently unraveled with every massive knot and jumbled snarl removed. In the end, we see a beautiful tapestry woven by the very string that we once considered unusable. The tapestry is the epitome of things worked together for good. It gloriously displays the hope, beauty, and significance generated by the trials we once wished to elude.

God did amazing things in Persia, and he is as active in our lives today as he was in Queen Esther's. Through our chaos, God communicates order and displays his sovereignty. Through our difficulties, God demonstrates his blessing and favor. Through seeming defeat, God delivers us, his children. He rescues the vanquished and overwhelms us with triumph. As we lean on him, he makes us victorious!

> *God is as active in our lives today as*
> *he was in Queen Esther's.*

Today, as we face our trials, let's meet them head-on with the confidence and assurance of our faith. For we know that when our trials feel like deep water that we must pass through, God will not allow them to overwhelm us. When our struggles feel like walking through fire, the flame will not burn. He has called us by name. We are his. (See Isa. 43:1–2.)

Like Esther, let's walk through our trials instead of around them. Let's press on instead of falling back. And let's cling to hope rather than surrendering to defeat. For we too have come to our current positions for such a time as this. Great things are possible when we walk in God's strength, and we too will be victorious!

There is great victory in the book of Esther, and it serves as an inspirational reminder throughout the generations. Before we dig deeper, read Psalm 116:12–13. Think through the victories in your own life and the memorial stones that you have established to commemorate their significance. We are well advised to hold fast to the victories that the Lord provides. I pray the Lord will help us all to teach future generations about what he has done for us.

Digging Deeper

1. Why do you believe that every nationality began to fear the Jews (Est. 8:17, 9:2)? Perhaps the following cross references will help your reasoning:

- Genesis 35:5

- Deuteronomy 2:25, 11:25

- Joshua 2:8–11, 5:1, 9:24

2. When it comes to Persia, do you believe that the Jews followed the counsel of the Lord in Jeremiah 29:7? Why or why not?

3. Why, from a military perspective, might Esther have asked for a second day to carry out the law (Est. 9:13)?

- Where in Persia might Haman have had his greatest level of influence? Could his influence have played into Esther's request?

- Could that be why Esther asked for a second day of defense only in the province of Susa?

- What significance would the hanging of Haman's ten sons have had to those who opposed the Jews?

4. Read Esther 9:20–28, which records the details of Purim.

- On which days were the Jews to celebrate (v. 21)?

- Why did they celebrate (v. 22)?

- How were they to celebrate (v. 22)?

- Haman had plotted against the Jews by casting the _____ (v. 24).

- What happened when the matter was brought before the king (v. 25)?

- Why do the Jews refer to the celebration as Purim (v. 26)?

- For how many years were the Jews instructed to observe Purim (v. 27)?

- Who is to celebrate the days of Purim (v. 28)? Was it intended just for Esther's time?

- Why is Purim observed (v. 28)?

5. Thinking back to the history of the Persian Empire, the armies of King Ahasuerus had suffered staggering defeat against the Greeks. When Haman offered 375 tons of silver to the royal treasury in exchange for eliminating the Jews (Est. 3:9), it's likely that he knew the kingdom was in financial straits. How does Esther 10:1 support this thinking?

6. Do you believe that it was the king's idea or Mordecai's to impose a tax and eliminate the need for war and plunder to fund the royal treasury? What examples from the book of Esther support your opinion?

7. What do we learn about Mordecai in Esther 10?

8. How did Mordecai's leadership differ from Haman's? Support your answers with Scripture.

9. As you read and meditated on Scripture, what insights did you gain that you can apply to your life? What promptings did you feel from the Holy Spirit as you studied?

Points to Ponder

Are you ready for a few interesting rabbit trails?

First, I invite you to do some Internet research on the Feast of Purim. What types of things transpire during this Jewish tradition? What symbolism is involved? How has it become more of a pagan holiday than originally intended?

Next, it's interesting to see how Esther appears in world events. Israel's President Netanyahu addressed a joint meeting of the US Congress on March 3, 2015. If time allows and if you're interested, I encourage you to read the transcript of his speech here:

http://www.washingtonpost.com/blogs/post-politics/wp/2015/03/03/full-text-netanyahus-address-to-congress/

Here's a small excerpt that might pique your curiosity:

"We're an ancient people. In our nearly 4,000 years of history, many have tried repeatedly to destroy the Jewish people. Tomorrow night, on the Jewish holiday of Purim, we'll read the Book of Esther. We'll read of a powerful Persian viceroy named Haman, who plotted to destroy the Jewish people some 2,500 years ago. But a courageous Jewish woman, Queen Esther, exposed the plot and gave the Jewish people the right to defend themselves against their enemies.

The plot was foiled. Our people were saved.

(APPLAUSE)

Today the Jewish people face another attempt by yet another Persian potentate to destroy us. Iran's Supreme Leader Ayatollah Khamenei spews the oldest hatred of anti-Semitism with the newest technology. He tweets that Israel must be annihilated."

Yes, in every generation, including our own, the Jewish nation has an enemy who wishes to destroy it. We can trust that God will prevail. By God's might and in his perfect timing, the children of God will be victorious.

And in our trials, so will we.

CHAPTER 11

Before Good-bye

*T*his has been a roller-coaster type of journey. I expect that, like me, you've cheered, and cried, and lamented, and danced, and rejoiced through the account of Queen Esther, Mordecai, and the Jewish nation.

Through every twist and surprise, I pray that you witnessed the hand of God moving with stealth and precision as he protected the Jews. Together we watched the Lord prove himself faithful, demonstrating how he values his children and has provided for their well-being for all time. We too are his children through the blood of Christ. Know that the same care and provision God showed the Jews is ours to grasp for today. Wil you choose to embrace it?

I pray that you came face to face with Jesus Christ, our Lord and Savior, even in the midst of Old Testament writings. God points to Christ in every book of the Old Testament, and Esther is no exception. Through images and symbolism, the love of Christ is portrayed and transcends history to touch our very lives. May we grasp every ounce of the companionship, comfort, and guidance that he lavishes upon us.

But God. . .

As we finish this study and move away from Esther, let's not set her victory on the shelf. Instead, let's continue to allow the teaching and examples resonate from Persia to present day.

Many times, God seems absent, but when we look carefully we see his active involvement. In Esther we saw that. . .

As a gentle orphan taken from her home, Esther must have been afraid, **but God** protected her and provided for her safety.

Haman had evil intent paired with the power to annihilate an entire race of people, **but God** intervened.

Esther was required to risk her life to approach the king on behalf of her people, **but God** provided for her protection.

Mordecai's heroic act was overlooked, **but God** made sure the king couldn't sleep and so remembered.

The king's edict to attack the Jews could not be overturned, **but God** ordained that the Jews could defend themselves.

In our own lives, perhaps we feel that . . .

- Our situations are too big to overcome

- Our families are on the cusp of falling apart

- Health concerns are bringing fear and anxiety

- Our job situations are in jeopardy

- Finances are tanking quickly

- God asks more of us than we believe we can give

In each of these issues, along with the thousands of scenarios I neglected to name, we can continue the sentence with the words "**but God** . . ."

He is our rescuer (Ps. 82:4), our provider (Phil 4:19, 1 Tim. 6:17), our protector (Isa. 41:10), our comforter (2 Cor. 1:4), our healer (Ps. 103:3), our friend (John 15:14–15), our teacher (John 14:26), and the true source of our identity (Gen. 1:27, Gal. 3:27–28). When we look to anything **but God** to fill any of those needs, we're looking in the wrong place. He alone is our source of all good things. He alone is faithful to provide all that we need.

As we close the book of Esther, let's commit to a lifetime of devotion to God and learning through the Word. Longing for God isn't what transforms us. Wishing he would do something isn't a life-changing exercise. We must commit to a life of seeking him, building relationship with him through time in his Word and prayer, and growing in trust that he will provide his best for every one of life's trials. Victory is coming in the Lord's perfect timing, whether on this side of eternity or the next.

The Lord is not some far-away, unapproachable deity. Quite the opposite is true. He wants us close to him. His Word tells us that he wants us close to him. He draws us near. See for yourself:

- Psalm 65:4 "How happy is the one You choose and bring near to live in Your courts! We will be satisfied with the goodness of Your house, the holiness of Your temple."

- Psalm 145:18 "The Lord is near to all who call out to Him, all who call out to Him with integrity."

- Hebrews 10:22 "Let us draw near with a true heart in full assurance of faith, our hearts sprinkled clean from an evil conscience and our bodies washed in pure water."

- James 4:8 "Draw near to God, and He will draw near to you."

Let's commit to taking him up on his word and moving into the nearness of God. Let's enjoy the process of finding triumph. Let's embrace our identity as children of God. Let's live like we're victorious—because we are.

> *Let's live like we're*
> *victorious—because we are.*

It has been my great joy to study victory through the book of Esther with you. Thank you for walking alongside me in such a rich and rewarding journey! May it bless you beyond measure.

Love,

Cathy

Leader Guide

Thank you for embarking on this study with a group of friends, family members, and sisters in Christ. Please know that I have personally prayed for you as you step into the role of facilitator and encourager.

Remember, the goal of any study is personal application and life transformation. We don't gather with the sole intent of growing in knowledge. Instead, we gather to spur one another along in our faith and help each other put what we learn into practice.

Victorious is formatted for group discussions that take place weekly over eleven weeks (an introduction session plus 10 weeks of homework and discussion). Each session can be completed within 45-60 minutes, making it perfect for small groups with tight time frames. If you are blessed with more than 60 minutes to meet each week, you can increase the depth of discussions, add time to enjoy snacks and fellowship, or pray over specific needs and requests within the group.

The First Steps

Prayer

Before you begin a group study, commit to pray for everyone you invite, for those who sign up to attend, and for unity within the group as a whole. Through your prayers, you will unleash the might of the Holy Spirit to minister to each guest in a personal and impactful way.

Seek the Lord's direction on which women to invite to your group. We can look at our contact lists and create a group on our own, but the Lord may very well bring to mind a quiet neighbor or co-worker that you haven't considered. Be sure to seek his direction and follow through, especially when you may feel uncomfortable asking someone you don't know well. It feels natural to ask those who follow Christ, but seek the Lord about inviting women who don't yet know the love of our Savior. This study might be exactly what she needs to hear before giving her life to the Lord.

Leader Qualifications

It's natural to have doubts as you begin to facilitate any study. You may have serious questions as to whether or not you're qualified. I'll remind you: in Christ you are qualified. Lean on the Lord and he will do great things through you.

It's important that as a leader you are a follower of Jesus Christ, desire a growing relationship with him, and have a heart for learning more about him through his Word.

As you lead this study, consider yourself a facilitator rather than a teacher. There is no requirement to be an expert on the Bible or a gifted instructor in order to lead the study. Your role is to guide group discussions and prompt members to share personal stories and what they've learned through their time in the Word.

Prepare to ask open-ended questions (for instance, questions that can't be answered with "yes" or "no") to stir on conversation within your group. The questions presented in the Digging Deeper and Points to Ponder sections will provide ideas and direction.

Communication

There are many ways to spread the word about a group Bible study: social media, church communication tools like newsletters and websites, emails, phone calls, and even text messages to those you know well.

Aim for three to four weeks of promotion and communication before the study begins.

Make sure that each woman you invite knows what to expect. Where will the group meet? What time will you begin and end? Will snacks be provided? Will there be child care available? Specify the items to bring along (for example, a Bible, a copy of *Victorious*, a journal for note taking, and perhaps snacks for one pre-assigned week of the study). Also provide details on how to sign up, how to get their book (I recommend that one person order books for the entire group) and the cost of the study.

Group Size

Small groups bring the best discussion and the most interaction when the group size is between three and twelve people. With just two people, unless they're close friends, it's hard to develop transparency. When the group increases beyond twelve people, not everyone feels comfortable sharing. Above all, let the Lord dictate your group size, but keep these guidelines in mind as you plan.

When the Study Begins

Ongoing Prayer

Now that the Bible study is starting, continued prayer is essential. Pray for each attendee at least weekly and as often as the Lord brings her to mind. Ask that the Lord do a powerful work through his Word, particularly as it relates to specific topics of the study and finding victory.

Leadership

It's important as the group facilitator that you lead by example. Be sure to complete the homework each week. Model the behavior of spending daily time in prayer and study of God's Word. Leadership is the process of influencing others and your strong example will encourage participants to develop good habits.

Set the expectation that group members complete the Digging Deeper section of each assigned chapter. They should also review the Points to Ponder section in order to prepare for group discussion.

The First Session

When your group gathers for the first time, you may want to introduce an icebreaker type of exercise. You might choose one of these simple ideas:

- Allow each member to introduce herself and tell a bit about her family, share what she enjoys doing, and what she personally hopes to gain from the study.

- Or, break into pairs (if you have an odd number of people in the group, the leader can sit out or form one group of three). Allow ten minutes for each pair to discuss the information requested in the first bullet point, above. Then, when the group reconvenes, have each woman introduce her partner and share the details she learned.

- Instead, and particularly if your group is already acquainted with one another, you might pose the following fun questions (providing options makes it easier for everyone to participate):

  o Explain a time when you had to eat disgusting food and still appear polite or professional.

- o What is your funniest memory with your best friend?

- o What is the most unusual tradition in your family?

- o Tell us one thing about yourself that most people don't know.

This first meeting sets the tone for your entire study. Encourage weekly attendance, which helps the entire group gel and build trust. Help your guests understand that when they miss a session, everyone misses the insights and wisdom that only they can share.

You'll see that in Chapter 1, one of the very first assignments is to read the entire book of Esther. This is not an assignment to scrutinize the entire book, but to read it quickly as an overview. This is a critical piece of homework, whether you study *Victorious* on your own or with a group. Please emphasize this point to your group. It may feel like a daunting assignment, but ensure group members that it's a rather entertaining and simple read. Members should be able to finish the book in an hour or two.

Commit to confidentiality. Each group member will need to trust the group as a safe environment where she can show her real, vulnerable side. Trust won't develop immediately, but you can help it grow by setting the standard of confidentiality.

Set the expectation, too, that this is meant to be a fun, interactive, and life-giving study. Laughter is encouraged.

A possible time map for Session 1:

7:00   Guests arrive

7:10   Open with prayer. Ask the Holy Spirit to guide the discussion and be your teacher.

7:15   Begin ice breaker activity

7:35   Pass out books

7:40 Set expectations for study (see above)

- Homework

- Attendance

- Sharing

- Discovering life application (not just head knowledge)

- Confidentiality / Vulnerability

- Fun

7:50 Discuss homework for Session 2 and address questions

8:00 Optional dismissal time. If you choose a longer setting, snacks, fellowship, and prayer would begin at this time.

Continuing Sessions

It's important to remember that as the facilitator, your role is to maintain the direction and pace of the class. If you have strict time frames to adhere to, you'll want to choose fewer questions to review. Or if time allows, you can increase the number of discussion points.

It's always more prudent to allow time for the Holy Spirit to move among your group than to become slaves of the clock. Having said that, when women gather together, there are often family needs and pressing schedules that remain adhered to the back of their minds. Ask the Lord to help you find an appropriate balance between a set schedule and a format that allows freedom for the women you invite.

For Sessions 2–11, I recommend a very simple format:

- Open with prayer. Ask the Holy Spirit to lead your discussion and to be the teacher.

- Prayerfully choose a few of the Digging Deeper questions to discuss (you may choose to select those that brought the most personal insight).

  The final question of each Digging Deeper section is the same and should be covered every week. Don't be discouraged in early sessions if there isn't much interaction here.

  Help members recognize that they truly can and do feel promptings by the Holy Spirit through their time in the Word. Help them see how the Spirit moves among them through times of general discussion. The conversation will grow as sessions progress.

- Ask the group to share personal application examples of how each chapter has moved them into a deeper relationship with Christ.

- Review the Points to Ponder section and discuss each point as a group.

- Give direction for homework for the following week.

- If time allows, share snacks, fellowship, and prayer.

- Close the session in prayer and specifically ask that the Lord move to help each group member find victory in their personal situations.

I'm Here for You!

Through social media and technology, it's easier than ever to stay in touch while you study *Victorious*.

Please let me know if you're meeting with a group. I am honored to pray over you and your group of women. (If you'd like to share the first names of those attending, it would be very helpful and encouraging to me). My team and I are committed to covering your study group in prayer.

If you're studying *Victorious* on your own, the same offer applies! ☺ Please connect with me on Facebook, Twitter, via email, or through the Strengthened by the Word Ministry website.

Let's Connect!

- ☐ www.facebook.com/strengthenedbythewordministries
- ☐ www.twitter.com/cathymcintosh33
- ☐ cathy@strengthenedbytheword.com
- ☐ www.strengthenedbytheword.com

Notes

Finding Triumph

1. Chad Brand, Charles Draper, Archie England, Steve Bond, E. Ray Clendenen, and Trent C. Butler, eds. "Hadassah." *Holman Illustrated Bible Dictionary*. Nashville: Holman Bible Publishers, 2003.

2. Ibid., "Esther."

3. Robert S McGee, *The Search for Significance: Seeing Your True Worth through God's Eyes* (Nashville: Thomas Nelson, 2003) 10.

Chapter 1: The Powerful Hand of an Unseen God

1. Frederic W. Bush, "The Book of Esther: Opus non gratum in the Christian Canon," *Bulletin for Biblical Research* 8 (1998): 39.

2. John MacArthur, *Twelve Extraordinary Women: How God Shaped Women of the Bible and What He Wants to Do with You* (Nashville: Thomas Nelson, 2005).

3. "Purim Animated," Aish.com, accessed January 18, 2015, http://www.aish.com/h/pur/mm/Purim_Animated.html?s=rab.

4. *Veggietales Esther: The Girl Who Became Queen*, (Franklin, TN: Big Idea Productions, Inc., 2000) VHS.

Chapter 2: It Just So Happened

1. "G4795 – sygkyria – Strong's Greek Lexicon (KJV)," Blue Letter Bible, accessed January 15, 2015, https://www.blueletterbible.org/lang/Lexicon/Lexicon.cfm?strongs=G4795&t=KJV.

2. Charles Caldwell, *Ryrie Study Bible* (Chicago: Moody Publishers, 1995), 764.

3. "Xerxes I 'the Great' king of Persia," Geni.com, accessed July 1, 2016, https://www.geni.com/people/Xerxes-I-the-Great-king-of-Persia/6000000006078785713.

4. "H2534 – chemah – Strong's Hebrew Lexicon (KJV)," Blue Letter Bible, accessed January 15, 2015, https://www.blueletterbible.org/lang/Lexicon/Lexicon.cfm?strongs=H2534&t=KJV.

5. Manser, Martin H. *Dictionary of Bible Themes: The Accessible and Comprehensive Tool for Topical Studies*. London: Martin Manser, 2009.

6. Wilson, Kenneth M. "Providence." Edited by John D. Barry, David Bomar, Derek R. Brown, Rachel Klippenstein, Douglas Mangum, Carrie Sinclair Wolcott, Lazarus Wentz, Elliot Ritzema, and Wendy Widder. *The Lexham Bible Dictionary*. Bellingham, WA: Lexham Press, 2016.

7. Warren W. Wiersbe, *Be Committed (Ruth and Esther): Doing God's Will Whatever the Cost (The BE Series Commentary)* (Colorado Springs: David C. Cook, 2010), Kindle Edition, 78.

8. Brand, et al. "Sovereignty of God"

9. Daystar Television Network's Facebook page, accessed March 22, 2016, www.facebook.com/daystartv.

Chapter 3: Crowned and Snubbed

1. "H157 – 'ahab – Strong's Hebrew Lexicon (KJV)," Blue Letter Bible, accessed January 20, 2015, https://www.blueletterbible.org/lang/Lexicon/Lexicon.cfm?strongs=H157&t=KJV.

2. "H32 - 'Abiyhayil - Strong's Hebrew Lexicon (KJV)," *Blue Letter Bible*, accessed August 15, 2016, https://www.blueletterbible.org//lang/Lexicon/Lexicon.cfm?Strongs=H32&t=KJV.

Chapter 4: A Picture of Evil

1. Wiersbe, *Be Committed*, 109.

2. "H2534 – chemah – Strong's Hebrew Lexicon (KJV)," *Blue Letter Bible*, accessed January 15, 2015, https://www.blueletterbible.org/lang/Lexicon/Lexicon.cfm?strongs=H2534&t=KJV.

3. "H8045 - shamad - Strong's Hebrew Lexicon (KJV)," *Blue Letter Bible*, accessed August 15, 2016, https://www.blueletterbible.org//lang/Lexicon/Lexicon.cfm?Strongs=H8045&t=KJV.

4. A. Boyd Lutter and Barry C. Davis, *Focus on the Bible* (Grand Rapids, MI: Baker Book House, 1995), 205.

Chapter 5: Counting the Cost

1. Lord Sachs, "The Refusal to be Comforted," accessed February 21, 2015, http://www.aish.com/tp/i/sacks/181741291.html.

2. Ibid.

3. Donald S. Whitney, *Spiritual Disciplines for the Christian Life* (Colorado Springs: NavPress, 2014), 197.

4. Dr. Josh Axe, "The Many Benefits of Fasting" accessed July 28, 2016, https://draxe.com/the-many-benefits-of-fasting/.

Chapter 6: Come

1. "H6944 - qodesh - Strong's Hebrew Lexicon (KJV)," *Blue Letter Bible*, accessed February 27, 2016, https://www.blueletterbible.org//lang/Lexicon/Lexicon.cfm?Strongs=H6944&t=KJV.

Chapter 7: The Game Changer

1. Wiersbe, *Be Committed*, 152.

2. Sheila Walsh, *The Longing in Me: A Study in the Life of David* (Nashville: Nelson Books, 2016), 109.

3. Wiersbe, *Be Committed*, 151.

Chapter 9: A King Who Provides a Way

1. Wilson.

2. Wiersbe, *Be Committed*, 175.

Chapter 10: Victorious!

1. Ibid., 167.

www.ingramcontent.com/pod-product-compliance
Lightning Source LLC
LaVergne TN
LVHW051415080426
835508LV00022B/3093